JOHN FITZGERALD KENNEDY
A Life in Pictures

Phaidon Press Limited
Regent's Wharf
All Saints Street
London N1 9PA

Phaidon Press Inc.
180 Varick Street
New York, NY 10014

www.phaidon.com

First published 2003
© 2003 Phaidon Press Limited. Text, images and layout © PHYB

ISBN 0 7148 4362 8

A CIP catalogue record for this book is available from the British Library.

Designed by Xavier Barral and Wijntje van Rooijen, Atalante
Printed in China

JOHN FITZGERALD KENNEDY

A Life in Pictures By Yann-Brice Dherbier & Pierre-Henri Verlhac

Φ

"We have the power to make this the best generation of mankind in the history of the world — or make it the last."

President Kennedy / September 20, 1963 / New York, NY / Address to the UN General Assembly

JOHN FITZGERALD KENNEDY, THE 35TH PRESIDENT OF THE UNITED STATES 1917–1963

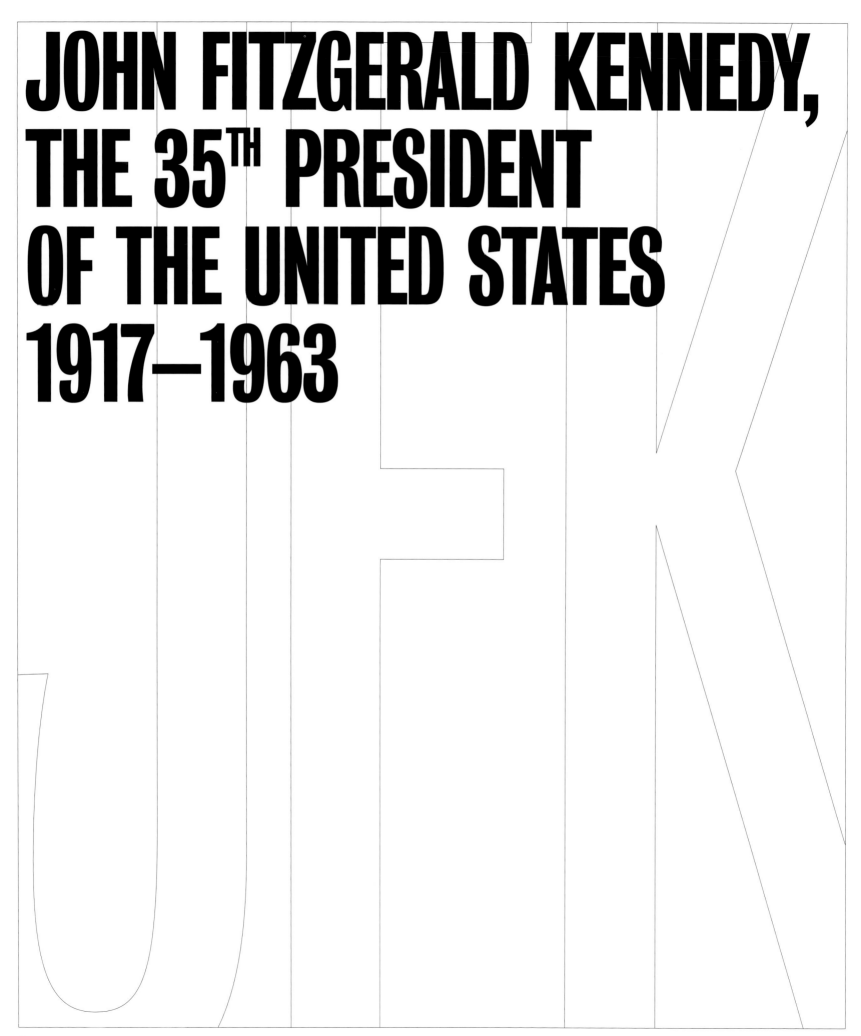

A GOLDEN CHILDHOOD

Born May 29, 1917, in Brookline, Massachusetts, John Fitzgerald Kennedy was the second of a family of nine children. He was named after his maternal grandfather. But, before long, everyone was calling him Jack. He was born into an Irish Catholic family with a well-established history in politics: his two grandfathers competed over many years for the mayorship of Boston.

His father, Joseph Patrick Kennedy, was a formidable businessman. A student at Harvard University, he promised himself that he would earn his first million dollars before he reached the age of thirty-five. At twenty-five, he became the youngest president of a bank in the United States when he took over the reins of Columbia Trust. Thereafter, he added to his fortune by succeeding in the stock market, motion pictures, the sale of alcohol, and real estate. At thirty-one, he made his first million dollars. In 1950, he was worth more than 400 million dollars.

Rose Fitzgerald Kennedy was an extremely attentive mother. Being a very religious woman, she was passionately devoted to her children and conscientiously recorded all the details of their lives in precious notecards, i.e. age, height, weight, shoe size, boo-boos, doctor's visits, communion dates and so on.

Jack, afflicted at birth with Addison's disease, which is a rare hormonal disorder, was a frail child who was often sick. He was on the brink of death in February of 1920, after having contracted scarlet fever, which lasted for several weeks. His brothers and sisters would often make fun of his illnesses, and would tease him, saying that a mosquito would have to be crazy to bite him: with his blood, the mosquito would have no chance of surviving.

Jack grew up surrounded by his three brothers (Joseph, Jr., Robert, and Edward) and his five sisters (Rosemary, Kathleen, Eunice, Patricia, and Jean). When he was eight years old, there were already seven children in his family. He led a privileged life in a luxurious house in the Brookline district of Boston, with twelve bedrooms and nine bathrooms. Rose looked after them with the aid of nannies and live-in domestics.

Beginning in 1928, the entire family would spend their summers at their home in Hyannis Port, Cape Cod. The property was an ideal location for engaging in different sporting activities (football, swimming, golf, sailing), and competition, encouraged by their father, often caused dissension amongst the boys. He had great ambitions for them and would incessantly repeat that they must excel in every activity they undertook, including athletics. In this field, Jack was the only son who could claim to steal the show from Joe, his elder by two years. However, Joe was very athletic and usually took the lead.

At the Choate School for boys in Connecticut, Jack surrounded himself with many friends, and was a diligent golfer, tennis, basketball, and football player. In school, he had a preference for history, English and literature. His friend, Lemoyne Billings, with whom he remained friends his entire life, remembers that from that young age, Jack was a subscriber to the *New York Times*.

In school, he didn't always study hard enough. His father was aware of this, and said to him, "After much experience in sizing people, I definitely know you have the goods and you can go a long way … that's why I am urging you to do the best you can." His professor would write, "Jack has a clever, individualist mind."

He graduated from Choate in 1935 at the age of nineteen, sixty-fourth out of a class of 112 students. During the summer, he studied at the London School of Economics, and was then admitted to Princeton University. Subsequently, he became seriously ill. The doctors considered leukaemia, then jaundice, and finally agreed on a blood infection. Jack left the campus before the end of the first semester and returned to Boston to be treated at Peter Brent Brigham Hospital. His convalescence lasted several months. Once back on his feet, he departed for Arizona to work with his brother Joe for the summer at the J Six ranch.

Upon his return, in the fall of 1936, he was admitted to Harvard University. There, again, his main focus was geared toward history and the arts, and he received average grades in his other subjects. His classmates were impressed with his passion for reading: he could read more than 1,200 words per minute and would devour ten to twelve books per week. He joined the football team at Harvard and was seriously injured during the course of a game. He had ruptured a disc, and this marked the beginning of terrible back pain that would follow him throughout his entire life.

After having been made president of the SEC (Security & Exchange Commission) in 1934, Joseph Patrick Kennedy was appointed the United States Ambassador to Great Britain in 1937. He moved to London with his entire family, except for Joe and Jack, who remained at Harvard. They corresponded with each other on a regular basis. Thereafter, Jack developed a profound interest in world politics and the politics of Europe in particular.

During the summer of 1937, he traveled throughout Europe with his friend, Lem Billings, and returned to Harvard more passionate than ever for world politics. At the time, Germany was being ruled by Adolf Hitler, and Italy by Mussolini. During the summer of 1939, he traveled to Europe once again. In September of the same year, Germany's invasion of Poland plunged the world into war. This became the subject of Jack's final thesis at Harvard University, in which he analyzed England's foreign policy, and its implications with regard to the Munich treaty of 1938. Published in 1940, under the title "Why England Slept," his thesis received favorable reviews from the critics and instant success in the bookstores. Several weeks later it had made the best-seller list.

In June of 1940, Jack graduated from Harvard. His father then sent him the following telegram: "Two things I always knew about you: one, that you are smart, two, that you are a swell guy. Love, Dad." He was subsequently admitted to the prestigious Stanford Graduate School of Business.

In 1941, America entered the war. Joe joined the US Navy as a fighter pilot and Jack attempted to enlist voluntarily in the Marine Corps in the spring of 1941. He was rejected due to his back condition. Through the end of the summer, he engaged in a personal and intensive physical training regime and succeeded in enlisting in the Navy in September. Being conferred the rank of lieutenant, Jack found himself entrusted with the command of a torpedo boat and a crew of twelve men.

Based in the South Pacific, he was given the mission of preventing the delivery of provisions to enemy ships. On August 2, 1943, his torpedo boat, PT-109, was sunk by a Japanese destroyer. As a result, Jack reinjured his back. He lost two of his men, but saved the life of Patrick McMahon, who was so seriously burned that Jack had to help him swim several miles to a small island. He spent many days searching for aid, and eventually happened upon two natives whom he asked to transmit a message engraved on a coconut to an Australian observation post located several islands away. On the sixth day, Jack and his men were finally rescued. Suffering from the spinal injury, Jack was transferred back to the United States and received the "Purple Heart" and Navy Corps medals for his acts of bravery.

ON THE WAY TO A POLITICAL CAREER

On August 12, 1944, Joe, Jr., was killed when a fighter plane that he was piloting exploded while he was engaged in a mission in northern Europe. Jack's destiny was henceforth significantly altered. He became the eldest of eight Kennedy children, and his entire entourage encouraged him to pursue the career in politics that had been promised to his brother.

Under heavy pressure from his family, and his father in particular, Jack conceded. Although he had aspired to teach or write, his father convinced him to run for a seat in Congress. Thus, a political career was born. He became involved in an intensely disputed campaign against nine other candidates and won by a large margin in the election of 1946. He was only twenty-nine years old. He was re-elected to the House of Representatives for the 11th District of Boston in 1948 and 1950.

In April of 1952, Jack announced his candidacy in the senatorial elections and based his campaign on the slogan, "Kennedy will do more for Massachusetts." In November, he defeated his Republican opponent, Henry Cabot Lodge, Jr., by more than 70,000 votes. He became senator of Massachusetts at the tender age of thirty-five.

It was during this period that he met Jacqueline Bouvier, who was introduced to him by a journalist by the name of Charles Bartlett. At the time Jacqueline was twenty-three years old. Born of a wealthy family, she studied at Vassar, one of the colleges for the most socially prominent young women of America, and pursued her third year of studies in Paris. In 1951 she obtained a degree in literature from The George Washington University, then pursued a career in journalism. She was employed at the *Washington Times Herald* in 1952 as a photographic reporter. When she met Jack, he was America's most eligible bachelor. She interviewed him for her newspaper and their relationship quickly became serious. They made their first official appearance in public together in 1953, during President Eisenhower's inaugural ball for his first presidential term. Shortly afterwards, Jackie was sent to England to cover the coronation of the Queen. While she was in Great Britain, Jack sent her a telegram asking for her hand in marriage.

On September 12, 1953, they were married in Newport where they held a luxurious reception for more than 1,000 guests, then flew off to Acapulco for their honeymoon.

Jack's back problems began to worsen significantly. The pain was such that he had trouble getting around with crutches. In a very weakened state (he had lost up to thirty pounds), he decided to stop at nothing to resolve his problem and underwent two major operations in October of 1954 and February of 1955. Although his doctors only gave him a fifty percent chance of survival, the surgery was a success.

During a long period of recuperation, he wrote "Profiles in Courage," a book relating the story of eight American senators who risked their careers to defend their convictions. The book was published in 1956. It was John F. Kennedy's second literary success. He received the Pulitzer Prize for this work in 1957, the year that his daughter, Caroline Kennedy, was born.

After completing his convalescence, Jack returned to his normal daily activities in the Senate and dedicated himself more than ever to national and international issues. He fought against racial segregation and, in 1957, became a member of the much-coveted "Senate Committee on Foreign Relations." At the same time, he became involved, at his brother Bobby's side, in the "Rackets Committee," which fought against the infiltration of the underworld in business, Union crimes and embezzlement of funds.

In 1958, Jack was re-elected Senator of Massachusetts in a crushing victory: he won over 700,000 more votes than his adversary, establishing a record in the state of Massachusetts.

THE 35TH PRESIDENT
OF THE UNITED STATES OF AMERICA

John F. Kennedy, who was very nearly nominated for the position of Vice President in the 1956 election, decided to run for the presidency of the United States in the following election. He announced his candidacy on January 2, 1960 and received the nomination for the Democratic Party on July 13 of the same year. It was the beginning of an exhausting campaign during which he traveled far and wide throughout the country. The entire Kennedy family was ready for action, and set to the task of making their presence felt by visiting the maximum number of states. The campaign against Richard Nixon was afoot.

The initial polls gave the edge to the Republican candidate: 53 percent to 47 percent. The first of four televised debates was the turning point of the election, which brought the two adversaries face to face on September 26, 1960 in Chicago. Impressive before the camera and quite persuasive, Jack emerged as the more modern candidate. The political analysts praised his delivery, saying that he captivated his audience and that his presence on screen was extraordinary. The day after the debate seemed to prove the experts' analysis: a small majority who followed the debate on the radio gave Nixon the victory, while a crushing majority of those people who watched the televised debate thought that Kennedy was the more convincing presidential candidate.

The second major turning point came about at the end of the month of October. The Reverend Martin Luther King, Jr., had been arrested in Atlanta for directing a peaceful demonstration and was sentenced, in an expeditious manner, to four months of hard labor. Jack and Bobby intervened on behalf of the Reverend and convinced the judge to release him. News of the event spread throughout the African-American community and assured Jack of precious votes, notably in Texas and Illinois.

On November 8, John F. Kennedy defeated Richard Nixon in the most closely fought presidential election in the history of the United States, receiving 49.75 percent of the votes compared to 49.55 percent for his adversary.

On January 20, 1961, Kennedy took the oath of office and delivered a speech that will forever remain famous. The entire world remembers his words, "Ask not what your country can do for you – ask what you can do for your country." At forty-three years of age he became the youngest elected president of the United States and the only Catholic man to ever have held that position.

Just prior to the inauguration, on November 25, 1960, Jackie gave birth to their second child, John Kennedy, Jr. Thus, Jack was a fulfilled man when he moved his family into the White House in January of 1961.

The presidential couple decided to make this White House a showcase of American history and culture. Jackie herself supervised the redecoration and acquisition of furniture, antiques, and works of art. She presented the fruits of her labors to the American people in a live televised program. More than ever, the White House took on a life of its own. Concerts were held there along with luxurious evening parties. The Kennedys would invite poets, artists, musicians, authors, athletes, and actors. The children had also settled into their new home: Caroline and John, Jr., were provided with a play area, pool, trampoline in the garden, and a tree house. It was commonplace to see them frolicking in the halls or even playing in their father's office. Despite the apparent casual atmosphere, the White House remained a perpetual center of activity and theater of important national and international events. The United States and the Soviet Union were engaged in the height of the Cold War and arms race. One of President Kennedy's principal concerns was the risk of nuclear war, which weighed heavily on the citizens of the world. Tensions were multiplied between the two superpowers, and he knew that war would be devastating for the entire world.

Kennedy dedicated himself to his job without paying attention to time. Working from seven o'clock in the morning to eleven o'clock in the evening, he began the day by reading six daily newspapers, and would then hold meeting after meeting with his closest advisors concerning the hot issues of the moment. He surrounded himself with a multitude of advisors and specialists who were well recognized in their particular disciplines, calling upon them regularly with high expectations. However, his most faithful ally in the White House remained his brother, Bobby, to whom he had entrusted the position of Attorney General.

One of the first decisions made by President Kennedy was the creation of the Peace Corps in March of 1961, which still exists today. This program provides volunteers from the United States with the opportunity to travel abroad to offer assistance in areas as varied as education, agriculture, health, and construction.

Several weeks after the introduction of the Peace Corps, on April 17, 1961, the failed invasion of the Bay of Pigs took place. Planned by the previous government and approved by Kennedy, it was planned that 1,500 Cuban exiles supported by a flotilla of B-26s would overthrow the existing Cuban regime led by Fidel Castro. The operation was a fiasco. For John F. Kennedy it was politically damaging, and he was criticized from all sides.

In June of 1961, President Kennedy met Nikita Khrushchev in Vienna. The two men discussed the problems of disarmament, Germany, the situation in Laos, and nuclear weapons testing. Though they were unable to find any middle ground with regard to these issues, they agreed to maintain regular contact to discuss problems relative to their two countries and the world in general. Shortly after this meeting, the Russians began the construction of the Berlin Wall.

President Kennedy was equally preoccupied with the advances being made by the Soviet Union in the exploration of outer space. He asked Congress to approve a budget of more than 22 billion dollars for the Apollo project and announced on September 12, 1962, during a speech delivered at Rice University, that the United States would send a man to the moon before the end of the decade. Seven years later, his prediction was realized: On July 20, 1969, Neil Armstrong walked on the moon, reciting the famous words, "One small step for man, one giant leap for mankind."

On October 16, 1962, the American Central Intelligence Agency discovered that the Soviets were helping Fidel Castro construct launch pads for missiles in Cuba. They identified a cargo ship transporting missiles to Havana. This was the beginning of the Cuban Missile Crisis. The entire world held its breath. Kennedy ordered a total military blockade of the island. He would not concede or waiver from this decision. Three days later, Khrushchev ordered his ships to turn around and return to the Soviet Union. The world had been on the brink of nuclear war. The winner of this international arm wrestling match, Kennedy, came out of the crisis rejuvenated, and more popular than ever in the United States.

Regarding domestic policy, one of the most important issues that Kennedy faced was the problem of racial discrimination. Although the Supreme Court of the United States abolished segregation in schools in 1954, the stark reality was quite different. Segregation was still being practiced not only in schools, but also in buses, restaurants, movie theatres, and other public areas.

Thousands of Americans descended into the streets. There were riots. The President ordered the National Guard to escort African-American students at the University of Alabama, and spoke to the nation that same evening during a televised address to affirm his unflinching support for the civil rights movement and request that his countrymen put an end to racial segregation. "One hundred years have passed since President Lincoln freed the slaves, yet their heirs, their grandsons, are not fully free. This nation was founded by men of many nations and backgrounds ... on the principle that men are created equal", he said.

During the last week of June, President Kennedy set out on an official tour of Europe. His visit to Berlin was very symbolic. Not far from the Wall, he addressed tens of thousands of people gathered on Rudolf-Wilde-Platz. Cheered by the crowd he delivered an inspiring speech on freedom: "All free men, wherever they may live, are citizens of Berlin and therefore, I take pride in these words, 'Ich bin ein Berliner'." President Kennedy then traveled to Ireland, the land of his ancestors, where he spoke before the Irish parliament in Dublin.

On August 5, 1963, Jackie gave birth to their second son, Patrick Bouvier Kennedy. Born almost six weeks premature, he died two days later.

That same day, President Kennedy signed the Nuclear Test Ban Treaty in Washington, DC, by which the United States, the Soviet Union, and Great Britain agreed to put an end to atmospheric testing of nuclear weapons. This was the result of more than two years of negotiations and constituted an important step in the easing of Cold War tensions. Two months later, these nations increased the parameters of the agreement by forbidding the placement of nuclear weapons in outer space. Most of the great nations of the world later rallied behind the accord and co-signed the treaties.

THE LAST DAYS OF JOHN F. KENNEDY

On November 15, 1963, the President flew to Palm Beach to join his close friends and relatives at their family home. He visited Cape Canaveral on the 16th. The center for space research would be renamed Cape Kennedy ten days later. (Today it is known as the Kennedy Space Center at Cape Canaveral.)

On November 21, President Kennedy departed for Texas. On the schedule were visits to San Antonio, Houston, Fort Worth, Dallas, and Austin, where he planned to make several speeches.

On November 22, he arrived in Dallas. Accompanied by his wife Jackie and the governor of Texas, John Connally, he rode through downtown in a convertible limousine waving to the thousands who had gathered to cheer him. At 12:30 p.m. shots rang out, striking the President twice in the base of the neck and head and seriously wounding John Connally. John F. Kennedy was rushed to Parkland Memorial Hospital, where he was pronounced dead thirty minutes later. He was forty-six years old. The entire world was in shock. Most people still remember precisely where they were and what they were doing when they learned the news of Kennedy's death.

Several hours after the shooting, the Dallas police arrested Lee Harvey Oswald for the President's murder. He would be fatally shot two days later by Jack Ruby.

Accompanied by the entire presidential team, Jackie Kennedy returned to Washington on board Air Force One with her deceased husband's body. In the sky, between Dallas and the American capital, Vice President Lyndon B. Johnson took the oath of office and became the thirty-sixth president of the United States.

On November 24, John F. Kennedy's body was laid in state, in the rotunda of the Capitol Building where his loved ones and many others came to pray.

The funeral took place the following day. It was organized in minute detail by Jackie, who was inspired by the funeral of Abraham Lincoln. Over one million people lined the route as a horse-drawn casket bore the body to St. Matthews Cathedral and then to Arlington Cemetery. More than ninety dignitaries of foreign governments were present. Although the event was broadcast live on television, more than one million people came to pay their last respects to John F. Kennedy. Jacqueline Kennedy lit an eternal flame on her beloved husband's grave.

Subsequently, the Warren Commission was organized to investigate the assassination of the thirty-fifth president of the United States. Their report was completed on September 27, 1964 and held that Lee Harvey Oswald was the sole gunman. No link whatsoever was found between him and organized crime.

However, in 1979, a separate commission concluded, after a two-year investigation, that Lee Harvey Oswald was but a pawn in a major conspiracy implicating members of the organized crime world.

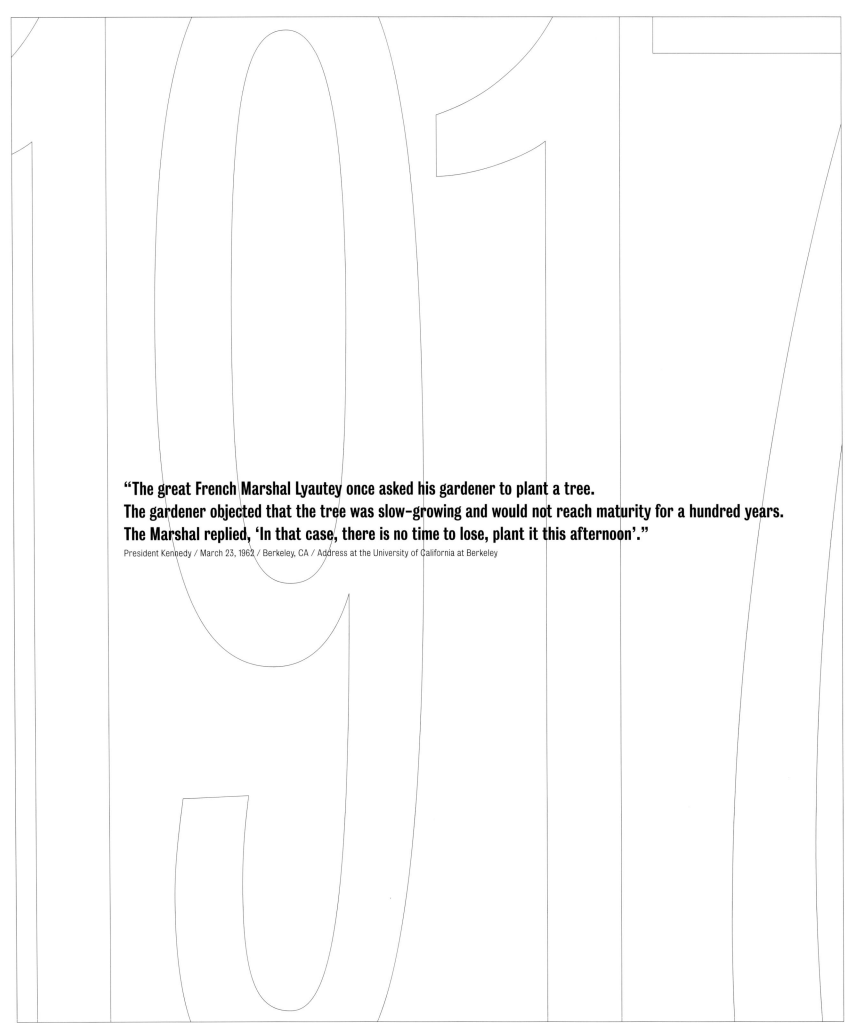

"The great French Marshal Lyautey once asked his gardener to plant a tree.
The gardener objected that the tree was slow-growing and would not reach maturity for a hundred years.
The Marshal replied, 'In that case, there is no time to lose, plant it this afternoon'."

President Kennedy / March 23, 1962 / Berkeley, CA / Address at the University of California at Berkeley

June 30, 1927 / Boston, MA / John F. Kennedy at the age of ten

1925 / Boston, MA / John F. Kennedy with his sisters Rosemary, Kathleen and Eunice

1925 / Hyannis Port, MA / The Kennedy children: Rosemary, John, Eunice, Joe, Jr., and Kathleen

September 1931 / Hyannis Port, MA / John F. Kennedy at the age of fourteen with his parents, brothers and sisters

1935 / Palm Beach, FL / Choate schoolmate Lemoyne Billings, Robert Kennedy, and John F. Kennedy

1934 / Choate, CT / John F. Kennedy while at Choate

1939 / Boston, MA / Portrait of John F. Kennedy

1935 / Boston, MA / John F. Kennedy on the day of his graduation from Choate

1928 / Boston, MA / John F. Kennedy, at the age of ten, wears the football uniform of Dexter School's first team

1936 / Boston, MA / Harvard swim team

1928 / Boston, MA / John F. Kennedy, detail from Dexter School first football team photograph

"A Plea for a Raise, by Jack Kennedy, Dedicated to my Mr. J. P. Kennedy

Chapter 1 : My recent allowance is $40. This I used for aeroplanes and other playthings of childhood but now I am a scout and I put away my childish things. Before I would spend $20 of my $40 and in five minutes I would have empty pockets and nothing to gain and $20 to lose. When I am a scout I have to buy canteens, haversacks, blankets, searchlights, poncho, things that will last for years and I can always use it while I can't use a chocolate marshmallow sundae with vanilla ice cream and so I put in my plea for a raise of thirty cents for me to buy scout things and pay my own way more around. Finis"

1927 / "A plea for a raise", a letter from John F. Kennedy to his father at the age of ten

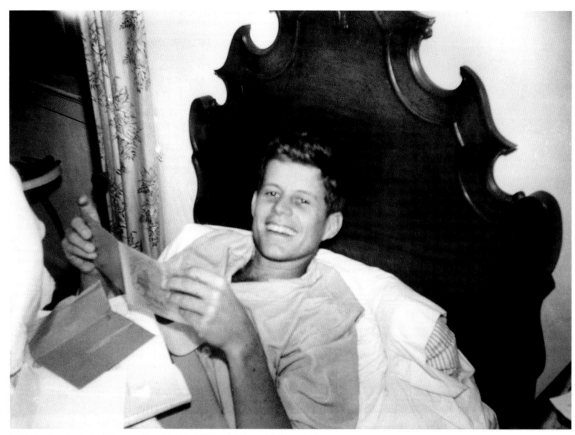

1937 / London, England / At the age of twenty, John F. Kennedy takes a trip through Europe

1937 / Venice, Italy / John F. Kennedy at Venice's Lido

August 1, 1937 / Franco-Italian border / John F. Kennedy

August 20, 1937 / Nuremberg, Germany / John F. Kennedy

August 15, 1937 / Venice, Italy / John F. Kennedy at St Mark's Square

August 8, 1937 / Mt Vesuvius, Italy / John F. Kennedy with two German soldiers (Georg and Heinz)

July 29, 1937 / Carcassonne, France / John F. Kennedy in France climbing Carcassonne's ramparts

1939 / Egypt / John F. Kennedy and a friend visiting the pyramids

August 24, 1937 / The Hague, Netherlands / John F. Kennedy with his dog "Dunker"
July 15, 1939 / London, England / John and Robert Kennedy watch as their sister Eunice leaves with her mother from the Embassy for Buckingham Palace where she is to be presented to King George and Queen Elizabeth

1939 / Boston, MA / John F. Kennedy at the age of twenty-two

1938 / Boston, MA / Joseph Kennedy with sons Joseph, Jr., and John

1941 / Boston, MA / Joseph Kennedy with sons Joseph, Jr., John, and Robert
March 8, 1940 / London, England / Joseph Kennedy while US ambassador in London

NAME	Kennedy, John Fitzgerald			RECEIVED S.B. DEGREE cum laude						Plan P		CLASS OF 1940	
CANDIDATE FOR S.B. DEGREE				Winthrop House								STATUS	
ADMITTED FROM	The Choate School, Wallingford, Conn. 1935			FOR PROMOTION	COURSES 4	C OR HIGHER 2	FOR PROMOTION	COURSES 4	C OR HIGHER 2	FOR DEGREE	COURSES 3	C OR HIGHER 2½	6-25-40 Bill not paid
										degree 4½-2			7-9-40 Bill paid

ADMISSION RECORD 1936-37   1937-38   1938-39   1939-40

68 - BC	ELEM.		ADV.		FRESHMAN	GRADES		Sophomore	GRADES		Junior	GRADES		Junior	GRADES	
SUBJECTS	UNITS	GRADE	UNITS	GRADE	STUDIES	Courses	Half Courses	STUDIES	Courses	Half Courses	STUDIES	Courses	Half Courses	STUDIES	Courses	Half Courses
ENGLISH		H			ENGLISH A Not Required			English F¹		C	Economics 61a¹		C	Economics 11b²		✓
GREEK					" 1	C		Fine Arts 1e		C	English A-1¹		B	" 62b²		
LATIN 1 yr					Economics a	B		Government 1		C	Government 7a¹		B	Government 3a¹		B
					History 1	C		History 32a¹		D	" 9a¹		B	" 4		B
GERMAN					French F	C		" 32b²		C	" 18¹		B	" 2²		B
								Government 30²		B	History 55¹		B	" 8a¹		B
FRENCH 3yrs			4	W										" 10a²		✓
											2-7-39 Leave of abs.			" 28¹		B
HISTORY Eng¹		H														
											PLAN O.K. for Honors 4/26/40 WEP					
ALGEBRA											PLAN COMPLETE 4/13/40 TKP					
GEOMETRY(PL.)																
GEOMETRY (SLD.)																
LOG. & TRIG.																
PHYSICS 1yr		W														
CHEMISTRY															DEGREE SUMMARY	
BOTANY														15.5		
ZOOLOGY					PHYS. TRAINING Satisfactory			F—INDICATES FRESHMAN COURSE						GENERAL EXAMINATIONS PASSED		

	GROUP NO. V	COMPL.	REQ'D	GROUP NO. V	COMPL.	REQ'D	GROUP NO.	COMPL.	REQ'D	GROUP NO.	COMPL.	REQ'D	History, Gov't and Economics.
Examinations under the New Plan.	COURSES	4		COURSES	8		COURSES	11	4.5	COURSES	15		May 1940
	C OR HIGHER	4	7	C OR HIGHER	7.5		C OR HIGHER	10.5	2.5	C OR HIGHER	15	11	RECOMMENDATION OF DIVISION
65-110	CHECKED BY	OK PWP TSM		CHECKED BY MHS	OK TSM		CHECKED BY			CHECKED BY			cum laude (Government)
	REPORT SENT	7-9-37		REPORT SENT	7-13-38		REPORT SENT			REPORT SENT			

DATE AND PLACE OF BIRTH May 29, 1917, Brookline, Mass.
FATHER Joseph Patrick Kennedy
MOTHER Rose (Fitzgerald) Kennedy
STREET 294 Pondfield Rd
CITY Bronxville
STATE N.Y.
SEND REPORTS TO Father 30 Rockefeller Plaza, N.Y.C.
Mother: also American Embassy, London

2-7-39-97 Granted leave of absence for the second half year in order to go to England.

VOTED BY THE ADMINISTRATIVE BOARD

REQUIREMENTS FOR DEGREE COMPLETED
CHECKED BY PWP
RECOMMENDED FOR S.B. DEGREE WITH
THE CLASS OF 1940
cum laude (Government)
RECEIVED DEGREE AS RECOMMENDED AT 1940
June 20, 1940
CONCENTRATION Government

LANGUAGE REQUIREMENTS READING
FAILED | PASSED
Jan 37 - March | Fr. F.: C

ADVISER:— Mr. E. P. Little   JUN 29 '37

CONCENTRATION OR HONORS:
_____ COURSES IN _____
OF WHICH MAY BE RELATED. _____ COURSES MAY BE OF ELEMENTARY
GRADE. THE PROGRAMME MUST INCLUDE

DISTRIBUTION:—

TUTOR:— Mr. A. B. Daspit   JUL 5 '38

CONCENTRATION OR HONORS:
_____ COURSES IN Government
OF WHICH MAY BE RELATED. _No_ COURSES MAY BE OF ELEMENTARY
GRADE. THE PROGRAMME MUST INCLUDE

DISTRIBUTION:—

TUTOR:—   MAY 29 '39

CONCENTRATION OR HONORS:
_____ COURSES IN Government
OF WHICH MAY BE RELATED. _No_ COURSES MAY BE OF ELEMENTARY
GRADE. THE PROGRAMME MUST INCLUDE

DISTRIBUTION:— Complete

TUTOR:— Prof. B. C. Hopper   JUN 13 '40

CONCENTRATION OR HONORS:
Complete COURSES IN Government
OF WHICH MAY BE RELATED. _____ COURSES MAY BE OF ELEMENTARY
GRADE. THE PROGRAMME MUST INCLUDE

DISTRIBUTION:— Complete

TUTOR:—

CONCENTRATION OR HONORS:
_____ COURSES IN _____
OF WHICH MAY BE RELATED. _____ COURSES MAY BE OF ELEMENTARY
GRADE. THE PROGRAMME MUST INCLUDE

DISTRIBUTION:—

TUTOR:—

Football - Swimming - Golf
Chairman, Smoker Committee
Student Council for 1937-38

JOHN FITZGERALD KENNEDY
Born May 29, 1917, in Brookline, Massachusetts. Prepared at The Choate School. Home Address: 294 Pondfield Road, Bronxville, New York. Winthrop House. Crimson (2-4); Chairman Smoker Committee (1); St. Paul's Catholic Club (1-4). Football (1), Junior Varsity (2); Swimming (1), Squad (2). Golf (1). House Hockey (3, 4); House Swimming (2); House Softball (4). Hasty Pudding-Institute of 1770; Spee Club. Permanent Class Committee. Field of Concentration: Government. Intended Vocation: Law.

VOTED BY THE ADMINISTRATIVE BOARD

DATE	TRANSCRIPT SENT TO	CHARGE
3-5-40	to Y.L.S. at K's reg	—
7-27-40	to Stanford Univ. K's reg	
3-31-41	to Yale Law - K's reg	31.00
8-6-41	to K - K's reg Navy	31.10
3-5-47	1 Cert. of Grad. to University Club of Washington — their req.	—
4-3-59	1 - self	2.50

02-Remington Rand Inc., 11 100-6381 5M 1935

II 3429

September 3, 1939 / London,
England / Joseph, Jr., Kathleen,
and John F. Kennedy walk to
Westminster to hear the British
declare war on Germany

1941 / Rio de Janeiro, Brazil /
Rose, John F. Kennedy
and his sister Eunice

January 18, 1944 / London, England / Lieutenant Joseph Kennedy, Jr., a member of the US naval forces that assisted the British coastal command in patrolling the English coast
March 28, 1944 / Boston, MA / Lieutenant John F. Kennedy, US Navy

June 11, 1944 / Boston, MA / Lieutenant John F. Kennedy is awarded the Navy and Marine Corps Medal and Purple Heart by Captain F. L. Conklin for his actions while in command of PT-109

1943 / South Pacific / PT-109 boat at sea

1942 / South Carolina / John F. Kennedy, while a lieutenant in the US Navy, based in the South Pacific as commander of a patrol torpedo boat, the PT-109

1941 / South Carolina / Lieutenant John F. Kennedy while serving in the US Navy

1944 / Hyannis Port, MA / John F. Kennedy, a friend, and his sister Kathleen

1944 / Hyannis Port, MA / John F. Kennedy with his sister Kathleen

January 1947 / Hyannis Port, MA / John F. Kennedy takes some time to relax after his election as a congressman for the eleventh district of Boston
1946 / Hyannis Port, MA / John F. Kennedy relaxes with his dog after winning the nomination for congressman for Massachusetts

1948 / Hyannis Port, MA / John F. Kennedy with his family (from left to right: Kathleen, Rose, Patrick Joseph, Eunice, Robert, Jean, and Edward)

1948 / Boston, MA / Rose and Joseph Kennedy with their children Eunice, John, Patricia, Jean, Robert, and Edward

1948 / Palm Beach, FL / Edward, Robert, and John F. Kennedy playing football in the garden of the family's mansion

1948 / Hyannis Port, MA / John F. Kennedy with his brothers and sisters

June 29, 1948 / Anacostia, DC / Senator John F. Kennedy visits the Naval Air Station of Anacostia with Captain Funke of the US Navy

July 1946 / Boston, MA / Congressional candidate John F. Kennedy speaks in front of a women's group during the primary election campaign

March 17, 1949 / Boston, MA / Evacuation Day Parade. From left to right: Hector Flaherty, Congressman John F. Kennedy, and Edward Connolly

1952 / Boston, MA / Representative John F. Kennedy campaigning for the Senate

"Our problems are man-made, therefore they may be solved by man.
And man can be as big as he wants. No problem of human destiny is beyond human beings."

President Kennedy / June 10, 1963 / Washington, DC / Commencement address at The American University

September 12, 1953 / Newport, RI / John F. Kennedy and Jacqueline Bouvier's wedding. They are surrounded (from left to right) by Robert, Pat, Eunice, Ted, and Jean Kennedy

September 12, 1953 / Newport, RI / John F. Kennedy and Jacqueline Bouvier kneeling in the century-old church of St. Mary's during their wedding

September 12, 1953 / Hammersmith Farms, RI / John F. Kennedy and Jacqueline Kennedy during their wedding reception attended by over 1,200 guests on the estate of the bride's mother and stepfather. Robert Kennedy is the best man

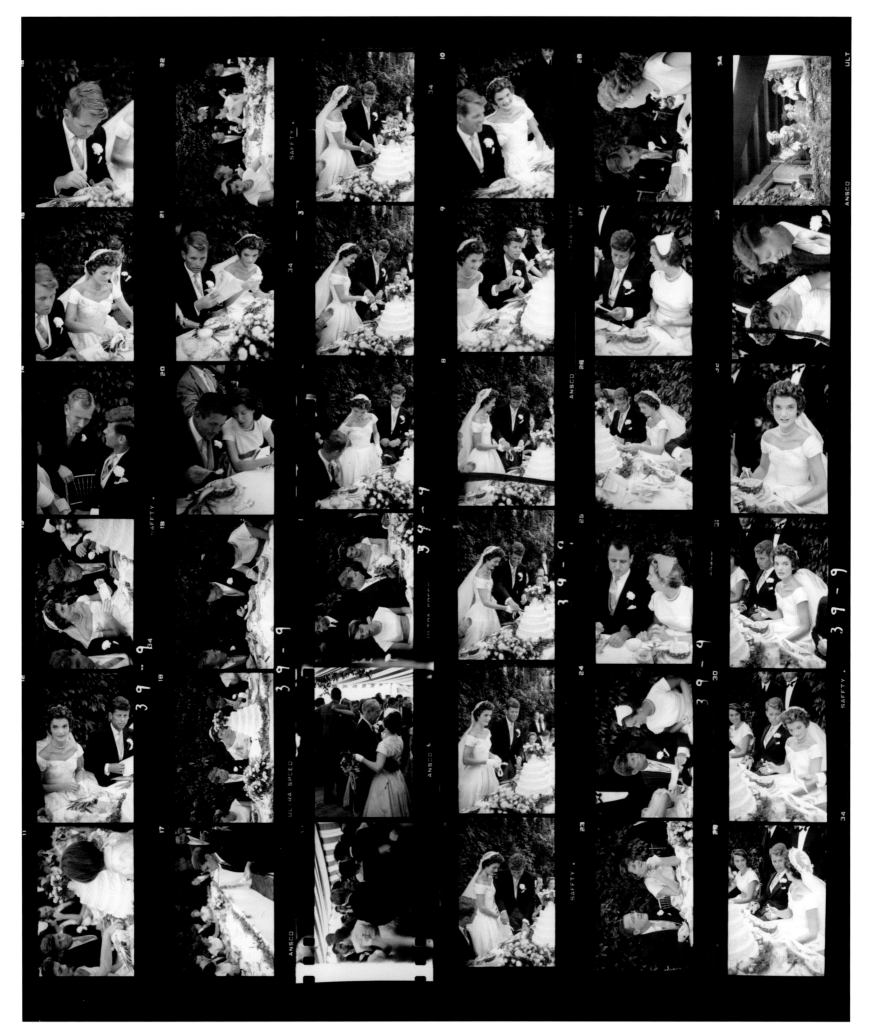

55

June 1957 / Hyannis Port, MA / Senator John F. Kennedy says goodbye to his wife Jackie as he prepares to leave Hyannis Port
c.1956 / Boston, MA / Photo booth portrait of John and Jackie Kennedy

Best of luck to John Kennedy Oct. 17, 1952 Harry Truman

October 17, 1952 / Boston, MA / President Harry Truman dedicated this photo to Representative John F. Kennedy, who displayed it in his Senate office
1955 / Offutt AFB, NE / Senator John F. Kennedy visiting the Strategic Air Command with General Tower (SAC Commander) and Senator Jackson

1958 / Washington, DC / Richard Nixon (thirty-seventh president of the United States), Rocky Marciano (former heavyweight champion), and Senator john F. Kennedy
c.1958–1959 / Washington, DC / Senator John F. Kennedy with Herbert Hoover, thirty-first president of the United States

Profiles IN Courage

DECISIVE MOMENTS IN

THE LIVES OF CELEBRATED AMERICANS

Senator John F. Kennedy

Foreword by ALLAN NEVINS

1955 / Original cover of *Profiles in Courage*, which recounted the stories of eight US senators who risked their careers, incurring the wrath of constituents or powerful interest groups, by taking a stand on unpopular issues. Senator John F. Kennedy received the Pulitzer Prize in 1957 for this book

1955 / Washington, DC / Senator John F. Kennedy writes at his desk in his Senate office

THE TRUSTEES OF COLUMBIA UNIVERSITY
IN THE CITY OF NEW YORK
TO ALL PERSONS TO WHOM THESE PRESENTS MAY COME GREETING
BE IT KNOWN THAT

JOHN F. KENNEDY
has been awarded
THE PULITZER PRIZE IN LETTERS
- BIOGRAPHY -
FOR "PROFILES IN COURAGE"

IN ACCORDANCE WITH THE PROVISIONS OF THE STATUTES OF THE
UNIVERSITY GOVERNING SUCH AWARD
IN WITNESS WHEREOF WE HAVE CAUSED THIS CERTIFICATE TO BE
SIGNED BY THE PRESIDENT OF THE UNIVERSITY AND OUR CORPORATE
SEAL TO BE HERETO AFFIXED IN THE CITY OF NEW YORK ON THE
SIXTH   DAY OF   MAY   IN THE YEAR OF
OUR LORD ONE THOUSAND NINE HUNDRED AND FIFTY SEVEN

PRESIDENT

1957 / Pulitzer Prize for *Profiles in Courage*. John F. Kennedy is the only American president ever to win the Pulitzer Prize

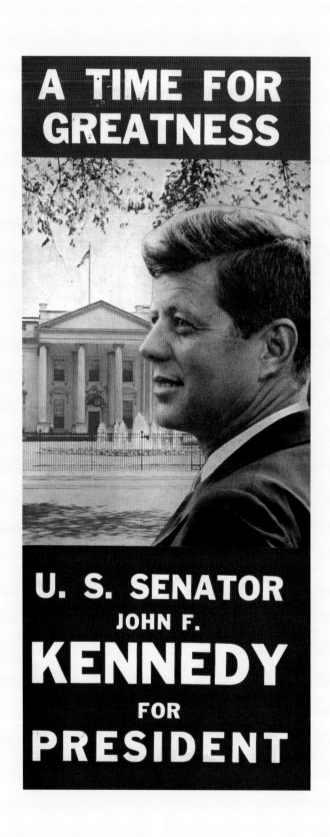

A TIME FOR GREATNESS

U. S. SENATOR
JOHN F.
KENNEDY
FOR
PRESIDENT

1960 / Presidential campaign poster

1956 / Boston, MA / Senator John F. Kennedy campaigning for his nomination as Democrat candidate for vice president, with Adlai Stevenson running for the presidency in the run-up to the 1956 elections

1958 / New York, NY / An elderly diner sits at a table above which hangs a poster for Senator John F. Kennedy's re-election campaign

June 6, 1958 / Washington, DC / Senator John F. Kennedy

May 1957 / Boston, MA / Senator John F. Kennedy

PAGES 69, 70, 71
May 17, 1957 / Washington, DC / Robert Kennedy and Senator John F. Kennedy, with members of the Senate Labor Rackets committee, during the sessions of the McClellan Committee, who were investigating underworld infiltration of companies and syndicate rackets

"IF MORE POLITICIANS KNEW POETRY, AND MORE POETS KNEW POLITICS, I AM CONVINCED THE WORLD WOULD BE A LITTLE BETTER PLACE IN WHICH TO LIVE."

Senator John F. Kennedy / 1956 / Boston, MA / Address at Harvard University

1960 / New York, NY /
Senator John F. Kennedy

April 1957 / Palm Beach, FL / John F. Kennedy and his brother Robert playing tennis in the garden of the family's mansion

August 19, 1960 / Santa Monica, CA / Senator John F. Kennedy surrounded by admirers as he takes a dip while spending the afternoon relaxing in his brother-in-law Peter Lawford's mansion

April 1957 / Palm Beach, FL / John, Edward, and Robert Kennedy at the beach

May 1957 / Washington, DC / Senator John F. Kennedy in his Senate office
April 21, 1958 / Washington, DC / Senator John F. Kennedy in his Senate office

August 4, 1959 / Washington, DC / Senator John F. Kennedy with brother Robert Kennedy

August 1959 / Washington, DC / Senator John F. Kennedy

August 1959 / Georgetown, Washington, DC / Senator John F. Kennedy

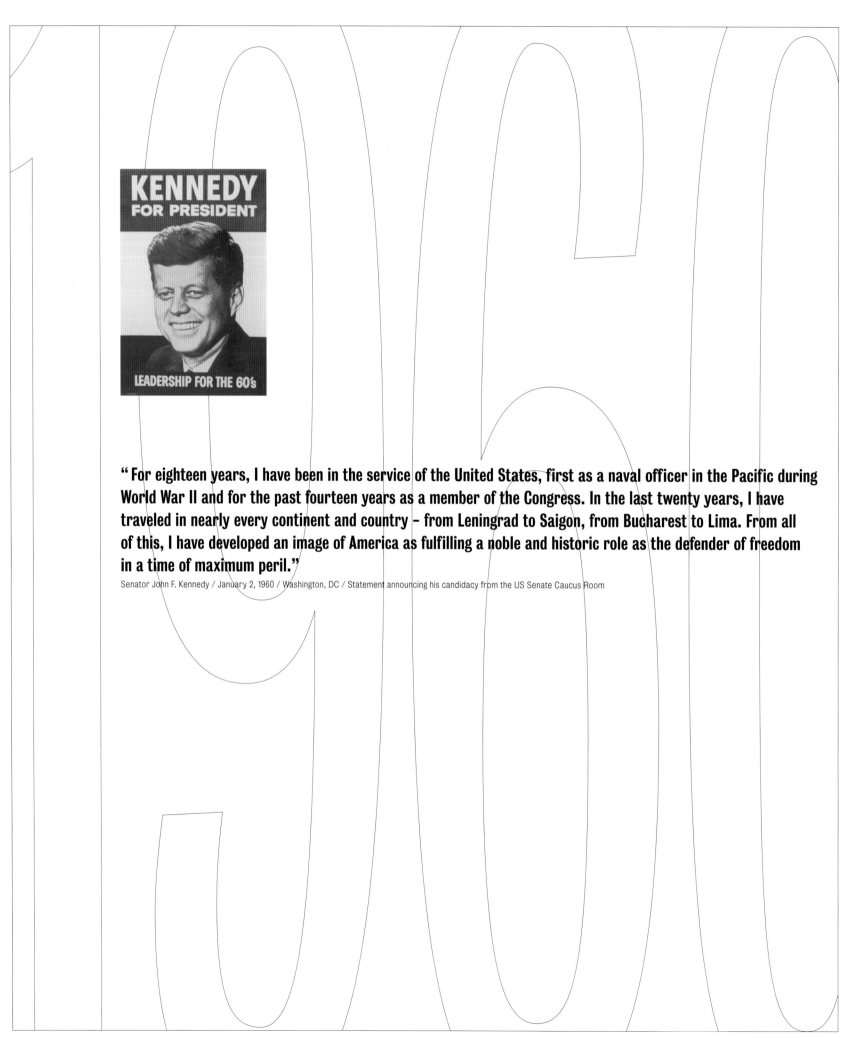

KENNEDY
FOR PRESIDENT

LEADERSHIP FOR THE 60's

" For eighteen years, I have been in the service of the United States, first as a naval officer in the Pacific during World War II and for the past fourteen years as a member of the Congress. In the last twenty years, I have traveled in nearly every continent and country – from Leningrad to Saigon, from Bucharest to Lima. From all of this, I have developed an image of America as fulfilling a noble and historic role as the defender of freedom in a time of maximum peril."

Senator John F. Kennedy / January 2, 1960 / Washington, DC / Statement announcing his candidacy from the US Senate Caucus Room

1960 / Presidential campaign poster
1960 / Unknown Location / Presidential campaign of Senator John F. Kennedy

1960 / Boston, MA / Wagon of the State Campaign Committee of Alabama

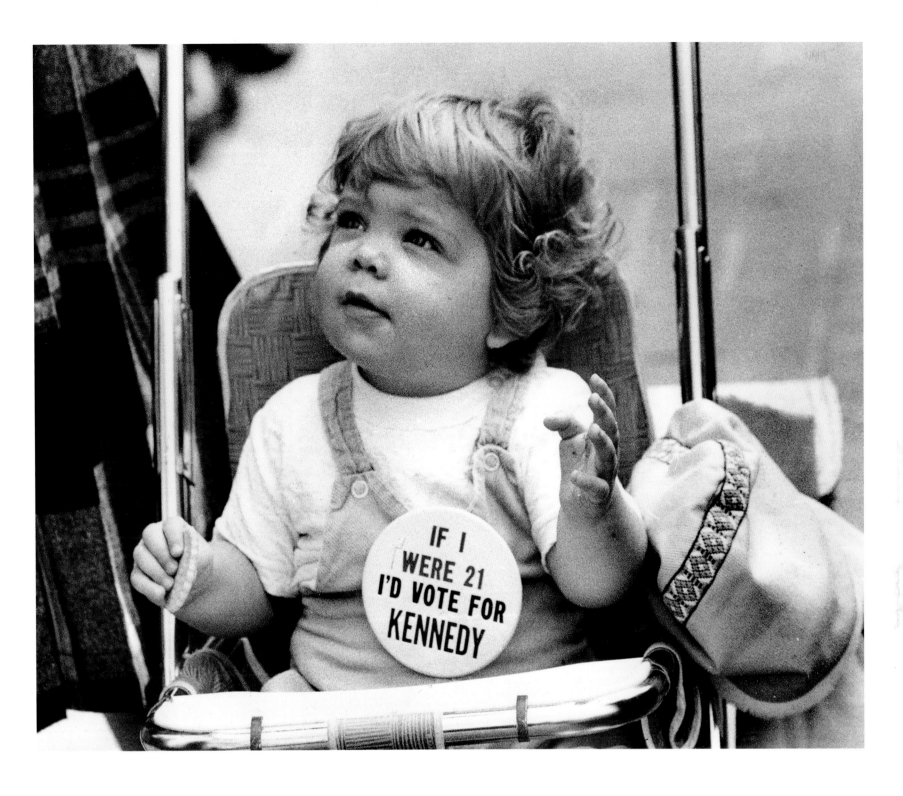

November 1, 1960 / Campaign button distributed during the presidential campaign

1960 / Los Angeles, CA / Senator John F. Kennedy acccepting the Democratic Party nomination for the presidency of the United States during the Democratic Party Convention
July 11, 1960 / Los Angeles, CA / Democratic Party National Convention at the time of the presidential campaign

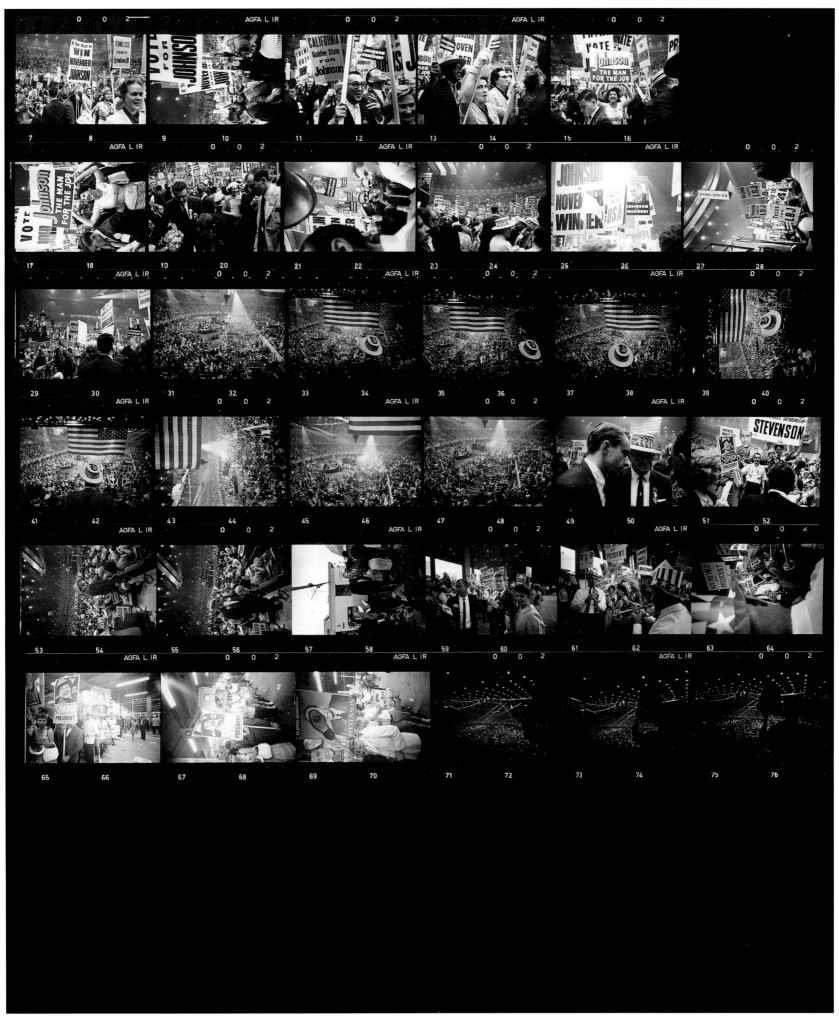

1960 / Washington, DC / Enthusiastic crowd during Senator John F. Kennedy's presidential campaign

1960 / Washington, DC / Evelyn Lincoln, John F. Kennedy's personal secretary, in her office

1957 / Senator John F. Kennedy reading

November 1960 / Chicago, IL / The famous debate in Chicago between Senator John F. Kennedy, the Democratic Party candidate, and Richard Nixon, Republican candidate, during the 1960 presidential campaign

1960 / Senator John F. Kennedy campaigning

"I DO NOT PROMISE TO CONSIDER RACE OR RELIGION IN MY APPOINTMENTS. I PROMISE ONLY THAT I WILL NOT CONSIDER THEM."

Senator John F. Kennedy / October 17, 1960 / Springfield, OH / Address at Wittenberg College

1960 / Senator John F. Kennedy in a plane during the presidential campaign

1960 / New York, NY / Senator John F. Kennedy campaigning

"LET US NOT SEEK THE REPUBLICAN ANSWER OR THE DEMOCRATIC ANSWER, BUT THE RIGHT ANSWER."

Senator John F. Kennedy / 1958

1960 / Unknown location / Senator John F. Kennedy campaigning

1960 / New York, NY /
Senator John F. Kennedy and Jacqueline
Kennedy campaign during a ticker tape
parade in Manhattan

1960 / Wisconsin / Senator John F. Kennedy
speaks in the auditorium of an elementary
school during his presidential campaign

1960 / Washington, DC / Senator John F. Kennedy campaigning

1960 / Washington, DC / Senator John F. Kennedy speaks at a podium while campaigning

"As Winston Churchill said on taking office some twenty years ago: 'if we open a quarrel between the present and the past, we shall be in danger of losing the future'. Today our concern must be with that future. For the world is changing. The old era is ending. The old ways will not do."

Senator John F. Kennedy / July 15, 1960 / Memorial Coliseum, Los Angeles, CA / Address while accepting the Democratic Party nomination for the presidency of the United States

February 10, 1961 / Washington, DC / Jacqueline Kennedy and her daughter Caroline leave the White House via helicopter for Glen Ora in Middleburg, VA

What your country is going to do
for you —   ask what you can do
for your country — my fellow
citizens of the world · ask not
                        or others
what America will do for you —
                         gives you
ask rather what you can do
for freedom. Both of you —
the same high standards of
sacrifice and strength of heart
and soul that we need from
you. ~~That~~ alliance for
~~...~~ with the finest

January 20, 1961 / Washington, DC / Draft of the inaugural speech written by President Kennedy ("Ask not what your country can do for you - ask what you can do for your country")
January 20, 1961 / Washington, DC / Senator John F. Kennedy takes the oath of office and becomes the thirty-fifth president of the United States of America. At the age of forty-three, he is the youngest president ever elected, winning by one of the smallest ever margins of victory, only 115,000 votes ahead of his rival. Lyndon B. Johnson, fifty-one, is his Vice President

August 28, 1963 / Washington, DC / President Kennedy with Attorney General Robert Kennedy (left) and Edward Kennedy at the White House

October 3, 1962 / Washington, DC / President Kennedy confers with Attorney General Robert Kennedy at the White House, West Wing colonnade

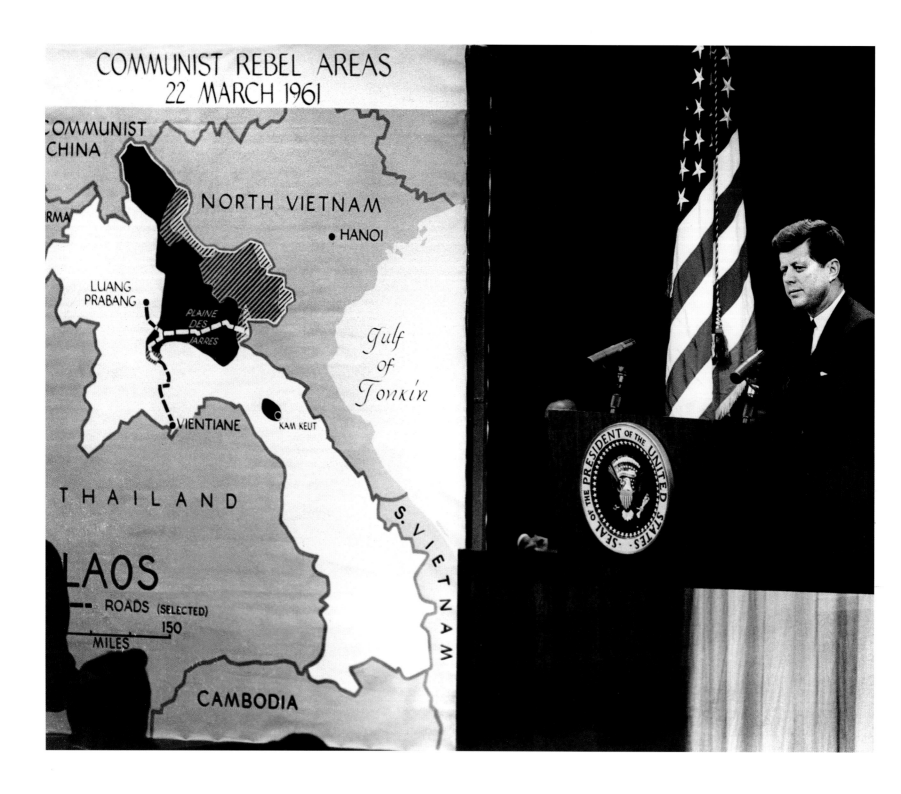

March 23, 1961 / Washington, DC / President Kennedy's eighth press conference with 426 journalists. Agenda: the rebel communists in Vietnam

March 21, 1963 / Washington, DC / President Kennedy at a press conference

May 3, 1961 / Washington, DC / President Kennedy and the First Lady at a welcome ceremony for the President of Tunisia, Habib Bourguiba

April 25, 1961 / Washington, DC/ President Sukarno of Indonesia has just taken off in his helicopter after a departure ceremony on the south lawn of the White House

April 10, 1961 / Griffiths Stadium, DC / President Kennedy attends the opening match of the 1961 baseball season. The Chicago White Sox are competing against the Washington Senators

April 10, 1961 / Griffiths Stadium, DC / President Kennedy throws out the first ball of the 1961 baseball season at the Washington Senators vs. Chicago White Sox game

LE FIGARO

Le Gaulois

achat et vente beaux livres anciens et modernes...

LARDANCHET
100 Faubourg St-Honoré · Paris 8e

0,25 NF
25 francs
Algérie
0,30 NF
30 francs

ÉDITION DE 5 HEURES

MERCREDI **31** MAI 1961

135e ANNÉE
N° 5.207
depuis la Libération

« Sans la liberté de blâmer, il n'est pas d'éloge flatteur. » — BEAUMARCHAIS.

DIRECTEUR : Pierre BRISSON

151e JOUR DE L'ANNÉE

Belg. et Lux. 3 fr. — Suisse 0 fr. 30 — Gde-Bret. 8 d. — Italie 50 lires

Tunisie 27 millimes — FR. M. 32 — Espagne 3 pesetas 50

LE PRÉSIDENT DES ÉTATS-UNIS
et Mrs John F. Kennedy
aujourd'hui à Paris

Premier entretien ce matin avec le général de Gaulle

suivi d'un déjeuner intime à l'Élysée

Propositions spectaculaires de « K » au Président U.S. attendues à Vienne !

Vienne, 30 mai. — Le président Kennedy et M. Khrouchtchev auront, à Vienne, dix heures d'entretiens : cinq heures le samedi 3 juin, et cinq heures le dimanche 4 juin, de 10 h 15 à 15 h. 15.

On laisse entendre dans les milieux diplomatiques communistes que M. « K » pourrait faire de nouvelles propositions spectaculaires, notamment à propos de Berlin, à l'occasion de cette rencontre. On doute, en effet, dans ces milieux, que le leader soviétique se laisse décourager par le simple tête-à-tête sans prendre une initiative quelconque.

Cet après-midi, à 18 h.
HOMMAGE
AU SOLDAT INCONNU

PAGES 8 ET 9 :
- l'article de Roger MASSIP
- la dépêche de Léo SAUVAGE (New York)
- l'ensemble de nos informations

WASHINGTON : N. CHATELAIN

Voici Kennedy

- Représentant de l'élite • Un animal politique encore inexpérimenté • Son entourage : les Harvard's boys

Washington, 30 mai. (De notre envoyé spécial permanent.)

LES terrains de la Maison-Blanche sont entourés d'une grille à claire-voie. Les promeneurs peuvent voir ce qui s'y passe. Les salons de la résidence présidentielle sont ouverts aux visiteurs quatre matins par semaine. Pendant la belle saison, la procession des touristes défile à travers les salons et la salle à manger, à quelques mètres du bureau et du Président travaille.

A toute heure du jour, on peut voir les curieux collés aux grilles, appareils photographiques pointés vers l'intérieur. A défaut des Kennedy eux-mêmes, ils peuvent toujours repérer surprendre la petite Caroline gambadant sur les pelouses, ou quelque chose que ses parents lui ont donné, le chien du Président ou la voiture de bébé, John Fitzgerald junior.

Les agents du service secret s'encouragent pas les promeneurs à stationner, mais ils ne peuvent pas les leur interdire. La Maison-Blanche, son contenu et la famille qui l'habite appartiennent au patrimoine national.

Le contribuable américain trouve naturel d'avoir un droit de regard sur les activités publiques et privées de la famille qu'il a contribué à installer là, grâce à son vote.

Au reste, les services de la présidence sont parfaitement conscients de leurs obligations à l'égard du public. Nous nommons patiemment, ainsi, sur l'heure des entrées et des sorties, des toilettes et de la couleur des cravates, des moindres changements apportés au décor intérieur.

Lorsque le Président réussit à disparaître pendant trois heures et qu'on se perdait ce qu'il ignorait où il se trouve, cela fait incendie et presque scandale. Quand il y a la messe, on nous le dit aussi, en précisant

le nom de l'église, celui du curé desservant et le thème du sermon. Ceux qui veulent tout cela ne prêt sont pas, par exemple, noter exactement le temps que M. Kennedy a consacré au golf depuis son entrée en fonctions et ont déduire à leur stupeur que le total dépasse celui d'Eisenhower pendant la période correspondante. Qui l'eût cru ?

La présidence américaine, chez les gens, est en somme l'institution la plus ouverte du monde. On sait plus sur la Maison-Blanche et ses occupants que sur l'Élysée, caché derrière ses murs et ses grilles aveugles, que sur le Kremlin et sur la datchas d'Gousoukalesloc et de Pitsounda, où réside M. Khrouchtchev.

La curiosité qui entoure les faits et gestes de la « first family » aurait été naturelle en toutes circonstances. Elle se trouve décuplée du fait que les Kennedy ne sont pas une famille présidentielle comme les autres. Ils sont jeunes — 44 et 31 ans, — ce sont, on l'a-t-on assez répété, sportifs, riches, beaux de parents et de grands-parents qui, eux aussi, avaient une fortune considérable : les Kennedy appartiennent à une élite. Les Américains n'ont pas l'habitude de faire des comparaisons peu flatteuses avec leurs prédécesseurs immédiats : seuls les Roosevelt auraient pu être classés dans la même catégorie. Mais l'élégance leur manquait et personne n'aurait attendu d'eux qu'ils impressionnent par leur style à toute ceux qu'ils impressionnent et prétendre.

Nicolas Châtelain.

(Suite en page 9, col. 2 à 6.)

CHALLE-ZELLER :
Jugement ce soir

Huis clos abandonné sur l'affaire Si Salah après accord entre l'accusation et la défense

- **LES GÉNÉRAUX DE POUILLY ET PERROTAT DÉPOSENT AU NOM DES LOYALISTES**

- Le général Valluy et le colonel de Boissieu disent **le patriotisme qui animait les inculpés**

PAGES 4 et 5 :
LE COMPTE RENDU D'AUDIENCE DE
JAMES DE COQUET

TEMPS PROBABLE
Assez beau, peu nuageux.
(Voir en page 16 les prévisions détaillées.)

Un récent portrait du président et de Mme John F. Kennedy.

Dans le ciel parisien, d'immenses pavillons aux couleurs américaines flottaient déjà hier.
Voici une vue de la Concorde ainsi pavoisée.

Pas de grève des fonctionnaires le 6 juin

- Accord entre les pouvoirs publics et les syndicats pour la restauration des traitements

- 180.000 petits fonctionnaires augmentés au 1er juillet de 20 à 30 NF par mois

PAGE 10 : notre information

Une toile attribuée à Rubens découverte à Chaumont

Chaumont, 30 mai. — Un tableau attribué à Rubens a été découvert à Chaumont, où un employé de banque amateur, qui fait le commerce l'occasion. Ce dernier, peu curieux, avait vendu le tableage de cette toile à 75 et 92 sur 0, 45 à un autre lampiste, estimé à Chaumont depuis quelques mois.

Un minutieux travail de décapage a tôt apparu une toile peu connue de qui recouvrait les initiales et les dimensions de l'œuvre. Dans un angle, une flamme du feu. Cette œuvre, dans le cadre de la bonne évolution de la souscription est sans aucun doute de la réel œuvre.

INCENDIE MONSTRE
dans le centre de Poitiers

Peu avant minuit :

Deux grands magasins sont la proie des flammes

- Une clinique évacuée
- Pas de victimes
- Dégâts matériels importants

(Page 2, nos informations)

Au large des côtes portugaises
UN D.C. 8 vénézuélien sombre dans l'Océan

avec 61 personnes à bord

PAGE 8 : nos informations

CHRONIQUE
L'ÉTÉ DE PICPUS

par Pierre GASCAR

J'AIME ce laconisme précis des guides (je parle, ici, des livres) : « Sonner et s'adresser à dr. à la concierge (rémunération) ». Les descriptions qui suivent me satisfont moins. Elles vous privent de la surprise et, devançant vos impressions, vous coupent l'herbe sous le pied. Il est bien entendu qu'on se croirait à cent lieues de Paris et que ce vaste enclos respire une paix villageoise, émouvante. Le second adjectif est de moi ; comment ne serait-on pas tenté de renchérir sur les appréciations du guide et d'ajouter un petit mouvement personnel à ses sentiments tout mâchés ?

Mais oublions les guides et laissons la mauvaise honte à laquelle ils m'incitent. Nous sommes à Picpus, dans les jardins des dames du Sacré-Cœur et de l'Adoration perpétuelle, au fond desquels se trouve un petit cimetière, et acceptons, une fois pour toutes, cette honte, aux lieux communs du cœur. Nous sommes entrés dans un autre âge, dans le silence du passé, le silence d'été de ces jardins de religieuses où poussent toujours de petites fleurs blanches un peu sucrées et où, dans une subtile odeur de miel, on croirait entendre le léger bourdonnement des vertus. De l'autre côté des plates-bandes où les carottes allongent avec les fleurs du mois de Marie, des religieuses, dont une coiffe godronnée entoure le visage, comme dans les portraits de la Renaissance, sont assises sous des socomores. Elles écoutent un jeune homme à la coupe de cheveux et à pâleur dénote qui parle, debout, mais qu'on n'entend pas.

On jurerait qu'il muet ou que, comme dans certains rêves incomplets, dans qu'un film privé de sa bande sonore, la vie se trouve réduite à une gesticulation lente, énigmatique. Symbolique, peut-être. Un peu plus loin derrière, au fond d'un bois pris dans les pierres de l'enceinte révèle l'emplacement d'une porte murée. De là, les charrettes criant, portant les corps des guillotinés de la place du Trône.

Il faut bien en venir à eux, si l'on veut comprendre l'étrangeté de ce silence. Quelque douze cents suppliciés, dont André Chénier et les carmélites de Compiègne, sont enterrés, au fond du jardin, dans deux fosses communes parfaitement nues et égalisées au ras du sol. Séparées d'elles par une grille, s'alignent les tombes de certaines familles des victimes de la Terreur, qui se sont rendues propriétaires du jardin même : la plupart de ces tombes sont couvertes de lourdes pierres grises, sans sculptures, d'aspect mégalithique.

Dans le jardin, le soleil, le silence, le vol bref d'un insecte, l'ombre des sycomores découpée sur le sol... C'était aussi l'été, alors. « Cette maison, jusqu'à le fort tranquille et ce désert, se trouva tort dérangée, trois enrollement surprise, écrit Michelet, quand, tout à coup, la commune, pour cause d'utilité publique, prit la moitié du jardin, l'entoura de planches, se mit à creuser ses fosses. » Cette décision provoqua d'autant plus d'émotion dans ces lieux qu'ils étaient occupés pas des prisonniers, le couvent ayant été décrété bien national et loué à un spéculateur qui en avait fait une maison de santé pour prévenus politiques des deux sexes. La liberté était extrême dans ces galantes prisons. On s'y aimait beaucoup. L'incertitude du sort rendait les cœurs tendres.

Là-dessus, le spectacle de la mort. De quelle mort ! Il faudrait recopier, ici, les pages, très belles, mais atroces, que Michelet a consacrées à cet épisode de la Terreur. Les relisant, je ne pouvais m'empêcher de penser à certaines dépositions qui sont faites, en ce moment, au procès d'Eichmann, à Jérusalem. Dans ces jours torrides de Thermidor, un architecte parisien avait proposé — il le prévoyait — le plan d'un crématoire pour les victimes ? Il y pensait, c'est vrai, les pilastres, les urnes, et il s'agissait d'hécatombes plus mesurées que de nos jours. Mais comment tout parler de mesure, quand justement la mort ne se mesure pas ?

Oublions tout cela. Il fait beau. Le silence règne sous les arbres. Tout est retrouvé. Paris est loin. Mais les hommes sont proches et les narrants inattendus de l'Histoire, ses vertiges. Ici, Michelet revient et le mot admirable : « Ce qu'on peut dire, c'est que l'homme qui semblait tourner cette roue (la Terreur), la moitié du jardin, l'entoura... » « A l'éblouir. Comment se fit-il qu'en 1961, me Picpus, cette image d'un jardin, son soleil, son silence, m'effrayèrent soudain ?

Pierre GASCAR.

May 31, 1961 / Paris, France / *Le Figaro,* leading national daily newspaper, runs as a headline: "The President of the United States and Mrs. Kennedy today in Paris"
June 2, 1961 / Paris, France / President Kennedy and the First Lady arrive at the US Embassy

"LADIES AND GENTLEMEN – I DO NOT THINK IT ALTOGETHER INAPPROPRIATE TO INTRODUCE MYSELF TO THIS AUDIENCE. I AM THE MAN WHO ACCOMPANIED JACQUELINE KENNEDY TO PARIS, AND I HAVE ENJOYED IT."

President Kennedy / June 2, 1961 / Paris, France / News conference in the Palais de Chaillot

June 1961 / Paris, France / President Kennedy

May 31, 1961 / Paris, France / Playing host at a state banquet at the Elysée Palace, French President Charles de Gaulle gestures at a refreshment table. Next to de Gaulle is the First Lady, wearing a new hair style, and President Kennedy
June 21, 1961 / Washington, DC / President Kennedy on his way to a meeting with the Prime Minister of Japan

June 4, 1961 / Vienna, Austria / President Kennedy and the First Lady boarding Air Force One, heading for England during their European tour

June 5, 1961 / Vienna, Austria / President Kennedy visits President of Austria Adolph Schärf
June 4, 1961 / Vienna, Austria / President Kennedy and his Soviet counterpart Nikita Khrushchev meet

1961 / Hyannis Port, MA / President Kennedy with his wife Jacqueline

1961 / Hyannis Port, MA / President Kennedy with brother Edward and respective wives Jacqueline and Virginia

1963 / Hyannis Port, MA / President Kennedy entertains a group of young Kennedy children with a ride in a golf cart

September 1, 1962 / Washington, DC / Jackie Kennedy and her son John F. Kennedy, Jr., in the nursery of the White House

1963 / Virginia / President Kennedy and
his wife relaxing at the weekend

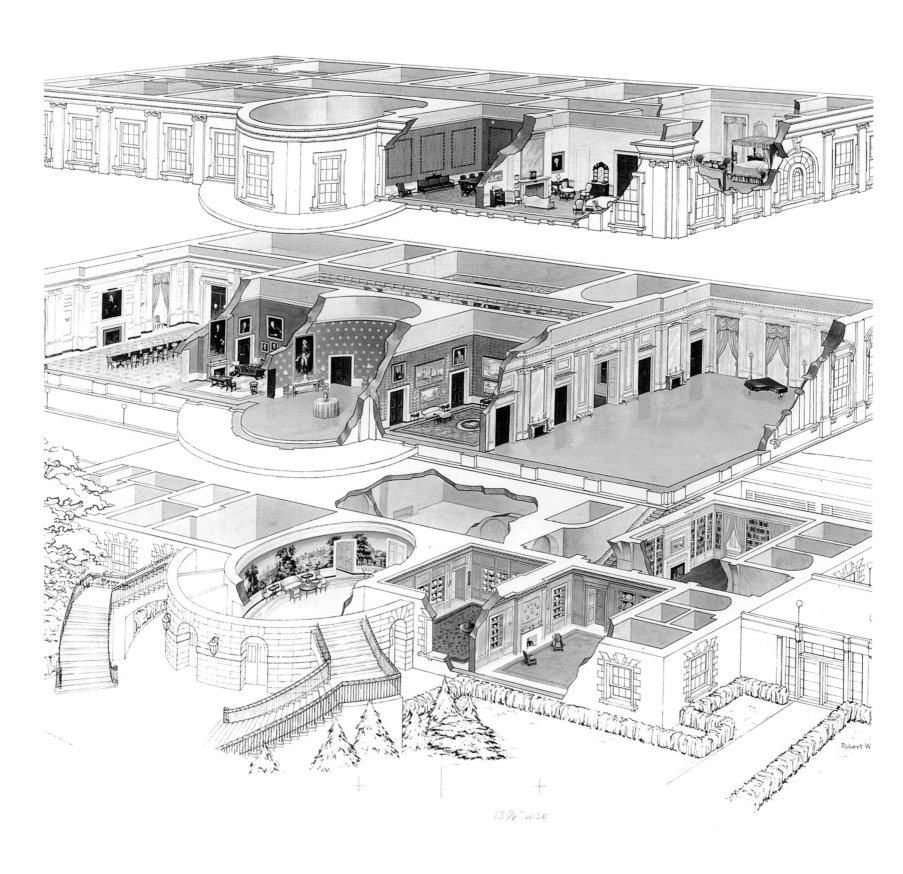

August 14, 1961 / Cross-section of the White House

May 8, 1962 / White House rooms: yellow oval room

May 5, 1962 / White House rooms: yellow oval room

May 7, 1962 / White House rooms: First Lady's sitting room

August 14, 1961 / White House rooms: Oval Office

August 14, 1961 / White House rooms: view from the presidential desk in the Oval Office

November 13, 1961 / Washington, DC / Cellist Pablo Casals plays in the East Room of the White House in front of 150 guests at a dinner honoring Puerto Rico governor Luis Muñoz Marin. That night, Casals played Mendelssohn, Couperin, and Schumann

November 1, 1961 / Washington, DC / Former president Harry Truman plays the piano at a dinner held in his honor at the White House. Music remained Truman's first passion after politics, and he often said that if he had been a good pianist he never would have become president. "I missed being a musician," he said, "and the real and only reason I missed being one is because I wasn't good enough."

August 1, 1963 / Washington, DC / A Secret Service agent watches President Kennedy taping two brief statements for television on school drop-outs and protection of marine life in the White House auditorium

September 25, 1961 / New York, NY / Address to the General Assembly of the UN

December 16, 1961 / Venezuela / Jacqueline Kennedy greets the crowds at La Morita, an agrarian reform site

December 16, 1961 / Venezuela / President Kennedy and the First Lady at La Morita. Jacqueline addresses the crowd in Spanish

"WE CHOSE TO GO TO THE MOON IN THIS DECADE AND DO THE OTHER THINGS, NOT BECAUSE THEY ARE EASY BUT BECAUSE THEY ARE HARD."

President Kennedy / September 12, 1962 / Texas / Address at Rice University

February 23, 1962 / Cape Canaveral, FL / President Kennedy visits the Space Center to present Colonel John Glenn with NASA's Distinguished Service Medal. Colonel Glenn shows the President the space capsule in which he traveled into orbit and circled the earth three times. The rivalry between the Soviet Union and the US was evident in competing space programs. It was President Kennedy who set the national goal of landing a man on the moon by 1970, a goal ultimately achieved in 1969

"I BELIEVE THAT THIS NATION SHOULD COMMIT ITSELF TO ACHIEVING THE GOAL, BEFORE THIS DECADE IS OUT, OF LANDING A MAN ON THE MOON AND RETURNING HIM SAFELY TO THE EARTH."

President Kennedy / May 25, 1961 / Special message to the Congress on urgent national needs

November 16, 1963 / Cape Canaveral, FL / Dr. Wernher von Braun explains the Saturn Launch System to President Kennedy. NASA Deputy Administrator Robert Seamans is on the left of von Braun

September 15, 1963 / Newport, RI / John, Jr., sitting on his mother's lap as President Kennedy drives a convertible car leaving Bailey's Beach in Newport for a cruise aboard the *Honey Fitz* in Narragansett Bay. Caroline is sitting behind her father

August 10, 1963 / Otis Air Force Base, MA / President Kennedy, accompanied by his sister-in-law, Princess Lee Radziwill, as he leaves hospital for Squaw Island

March 15, 1962 / Agra, India / Jacqueline Kennedy stands in front of the Taj Mahal, during her semi-official visit to India and other parts of Asia. Jacqueline was the first president's wife to make official visits without the president

March 17, 1962 / Udaipur, India / Jacqueline Kennedy with her sister Princess Lee Radziwill on a boat trip on Lake Pichola

March 17, 1962 / Udaipur, India / The First Lady in India
March 16, 1962 / New Delhi, India / The First Lady with the Maharaja of Patiala at the residence of Indian Prime Minister Jawaharlal Nehru

March 21, 1962 / New Delhi, India / The First Lady with Indian Prime Minister Jawaharlal Nehru

March 17, 1962 / Udaipur, India / The First Lady in India with her sister Princess Lee Radziwill, while visiting Lake Pichola. The American ambassador to India described Jackie Kennedy's visit as "wonderfully useful to us" at a time when the United States worried about Soviet interest in the region

"AND SO, MY FELLOW AMERICANS: ASK NOT WHAT YOUR COUNTRY CAN DO FOR YOU — ASK WHAT YOU CAN DO FOR YOUR COUNTRY"

President Kennedy / January 20, 1961 / Washington, DC / Inaugural address

PAGES 159, 160, 161, 162
February 7, 1963 / Washinton, DC / Shortly after taking office, President Kennedy started holding regular news conferences, televised live from the State Department auditorium. His easygoing style and quick wit instantly endeared him to many reporters and to the American people watching at home

March 11, 1963 / Washington, DC / President Kennedy leaves the State Department auditorium quickly after speaking at a press conference

pages 164, 165, 166:
May 11, 1962 / Washington, DC / Dinner in honor of the French Minister of State for Cultural Affairs André Malraux in the White House. He and Mrs. Kennedy were close friends and worked together to enable the exhibition of the *Mona Lisa* **in New York. It was the first time the masterpiece had left the Louvre in Paris**

January 8, 1963 / Washington, DC / Jacqueline Kennedy and French Minister for Cultural Affairs André Malraux at the opening ceremony of the *Mona Lisa* exhibit at the National Gallery of Art. Leonardo da Vinci's *Mona Lisa* was lent to the United States in 1963 thanks to Jackie's support. In André Malraux's own words: "There has been talk of the risks this painting took by leaving the Louvre. They are real, though exaggerated. But the risk taken by the boys who landed one day at Arromanches, to say nothing of those who proceeded them twenty-five years before, were much more certain. To the humblest among them who may be listening to me now, I want to say without raising my voice that the masterpiece to which you are paying historic homage this evening, Mr. President, is a painting which he has saved."

"WE MUST NEVER FORGET THAT ART IS NOT A FORM OF PROPAGANDA; IT IS A FORM OF TRUTH."

President Kennedy / October 26, 1963 / Amherst, MA / Address at Amherst College, in honor of poet Robert Frost

January 8, 1963 / Washington, DC / Jacqueline Kennedy with André Malraux, at the opening ceremony of the *Mona Lisa* exhibit at the National Gallery of Art

May 27, 1961 / Washington, DC / President Kennedy's birthday party celebrations at the National Guard Armory

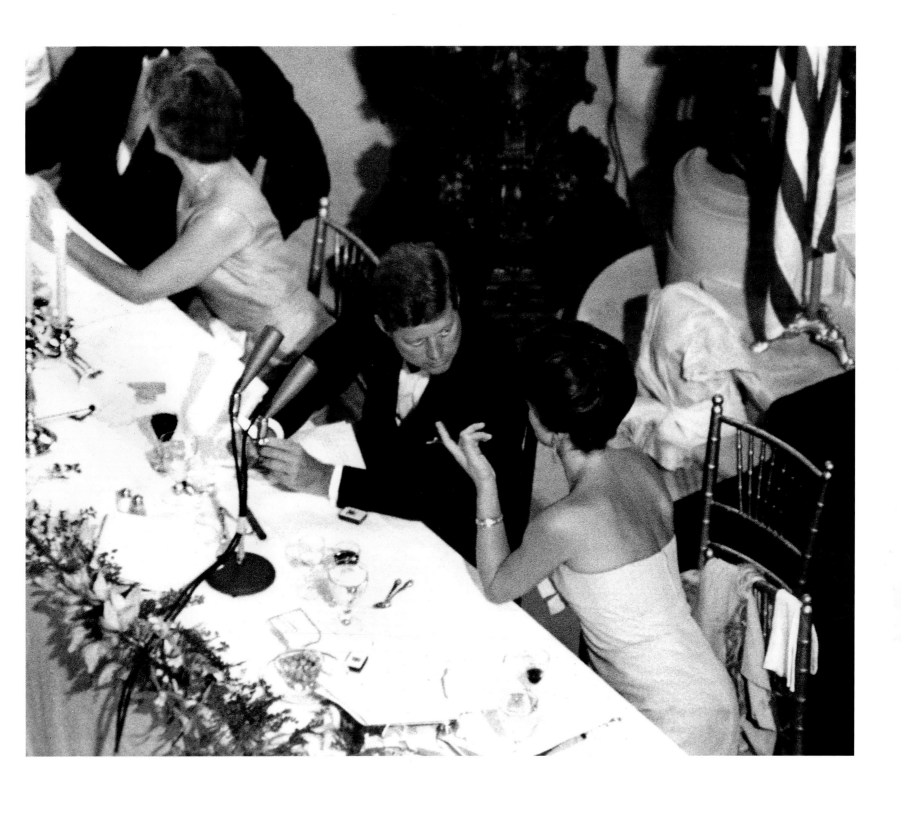

September 14, 1962 / Newport, RI / President Kennedy and the First Lady at an America's Cup dinner given by Australian Ambassador, Sir Howard Beale, at The Breakers mansion

May 19, 1962 / New York, NY / Maria Callas with President Kennedy at his forty-fifth birthday party organized by Arthur Krim with forty celebrities, including Marilyn Monroe

May 24, 1961 / Washington, DC / Princess Grace of Monaco and President Kennedy talk during her visit to the White House

May 19, 1962 / New York, NY / Marilyn Monroe at Madison Square Garden with her famous rendition of "Happy Birthday" for the President at a Democratic fund-raising dinner
July 20, 1960 / Hyannis Port, MA / John, Robert, and Edward Kennedy

July 20, 1962 / Washington, DC / President Kennedy meets with the French Finance Minister, Valéry Giscard d'Estaing, at the White House

March 26, 1962 / Washington, DC / President Kennedy receives Mrs. Indira Ghandi (daughter of Indian Prime Minister Jawaharlal Nehru) at the White House, with Mrs. B. K. Nehru, and Hon. D. N. Chaterji, Chargé d'Affaires at the Indian embassy in the US

PAGES 178, 179, 180
June 29, 1962 / Mexico City / President Kennedy and his Mexican counterpart Lopez Mateos in a motorcade along Avenida 20 Noviembre. President Kennedy made this trip to promote the Alliance for Progress, a plan for developing the economies of Latin American nations

November 5, 1962 / Rio de Janeiro, Brazil / Within a few hours of President Kennedy announcing the military quarantine of Cuba via a nationwide radio-television address on October 22, posters similar to the one shown above appeared suddenly all over this South American city. The sign states "Hail Kennedy, the defender of the Americas." In the background is Rio de Janeiro's main rail terminal "Central do Brasil"

October 10, 1962 / Washington, DC / Welcome ceremony for the President of Guinea Mr. Sékou Touré. Mr. Sékou Touré became the first president of an independent Guinea in 1958 and symbolized for many Africans the spirit of anti-colonialism

July 2, 1962 / Naples, Italy / President Kennedy greets the crowds in a motorcade on his way to Capodochino airport with Italian President Antonio Segni

1961 / Views of the presidential limousine SS-100-X, a dark blue custom-built 1961 Lincoln Continental stretch limousine designed by the Ford Motor Company. With the inauguration of a forty-three-year-old president, the first to be born in the twentieth century, a modern limousine was the necessary symbol of a new beginning. It was later repainted black at the request of President Lyndon B. Johnson. SS-100-X is kept at the Henry Ford Museum in Dearborn, Michigan

July 11, 1961 / Washington, DC / President Kennedy and the First Lady welcome the President of Pakistan Mohammad Ayub Khan, who is on an official visit to Washington to meet his newly elected American counterpart

August 9, 1962 / Washington, DC / President Kennedy meets Peace Corps volunteers at the White House before they depart for Africa. Shortly after taking office, the President created the Peace Corps, hoping to inspire young Americans to serve overseas in developing countries

September 25, 1962 / Washington, DC / President Kennedy and his wife after the première of "Mr President". Jackie saw the entire show, while President Kennedy joined her at the intermission

June 30, 1962 / Mexico City / President Kennedy and the First Lady visits the Instituto Nacional de Protección a la Infancia

May 5, 1961 / Washington, DC / In the President's secretary's office at the White House, President Kennedy, with Jacqueline and Vice President Lyndon B. Johnson, views the lift-off of astronaut Alan Shepard on the first US manned sub-orbital flight

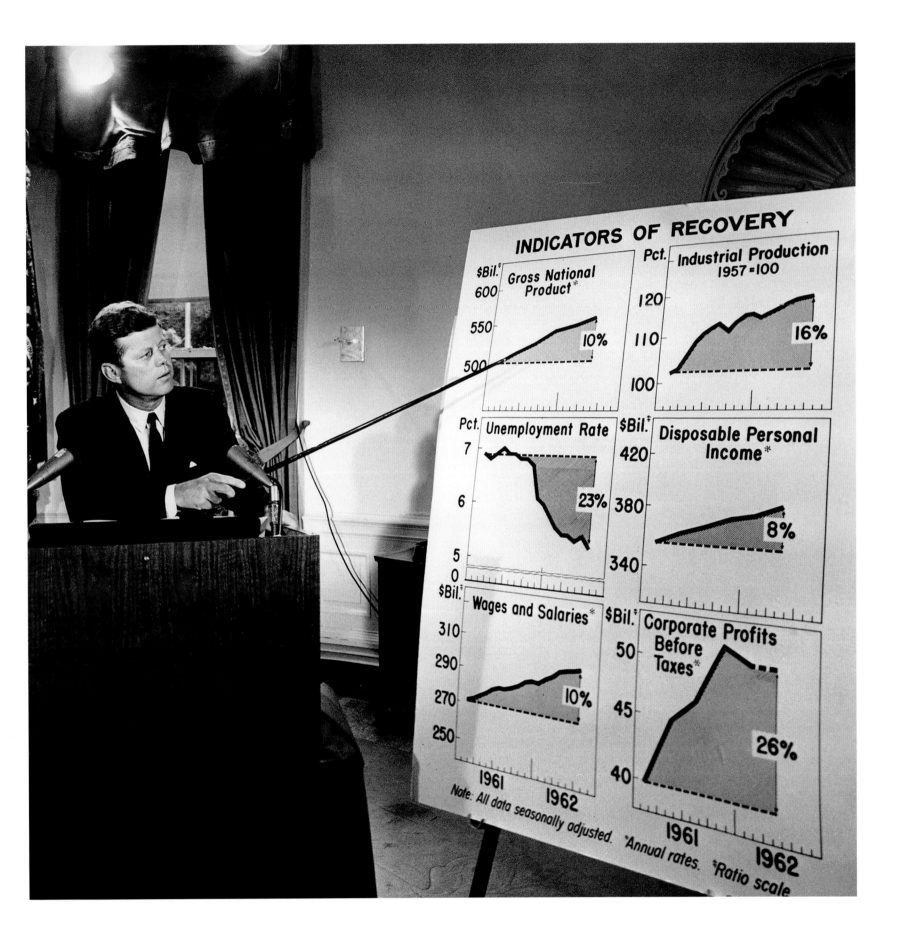

August 13, 1962 / Washington, DC / Live radio and television address to the nation from the White House regarding the state of the economy

August 31, 1962 / Quonset Point Naval Air Station, RI / President Kennedy with Jacqueline and young daughter Caroline on their return from a vacation in Italy

1962 / Washington, DC / President Kennedy with his wife and children Caroline and John, Jr.
August 21, 1959 / Hyannis Port, MA / Jackie Kennedy reads to her young daughter, Caroline

September 15, 1963 / Newport, RI / President Kennedy with son John, Jr., at the age of three

August 4, 1962 / Hyannis Port, MA / President Kennedy and Jacqueline with their children Caroline and John, Jr.

May 5, 1963 / Camp David, MD / Caroline Kennedy with Secret Service agent Foster, in charge of her security
August 31, 1963 / Hyannis Port, MA / John, Jr., plays next to a Secret Service agent who is looking after him

September 15, 1962 / Newport, RI / President Kennedy and Jacqueline watch the 21st America's Cup Race

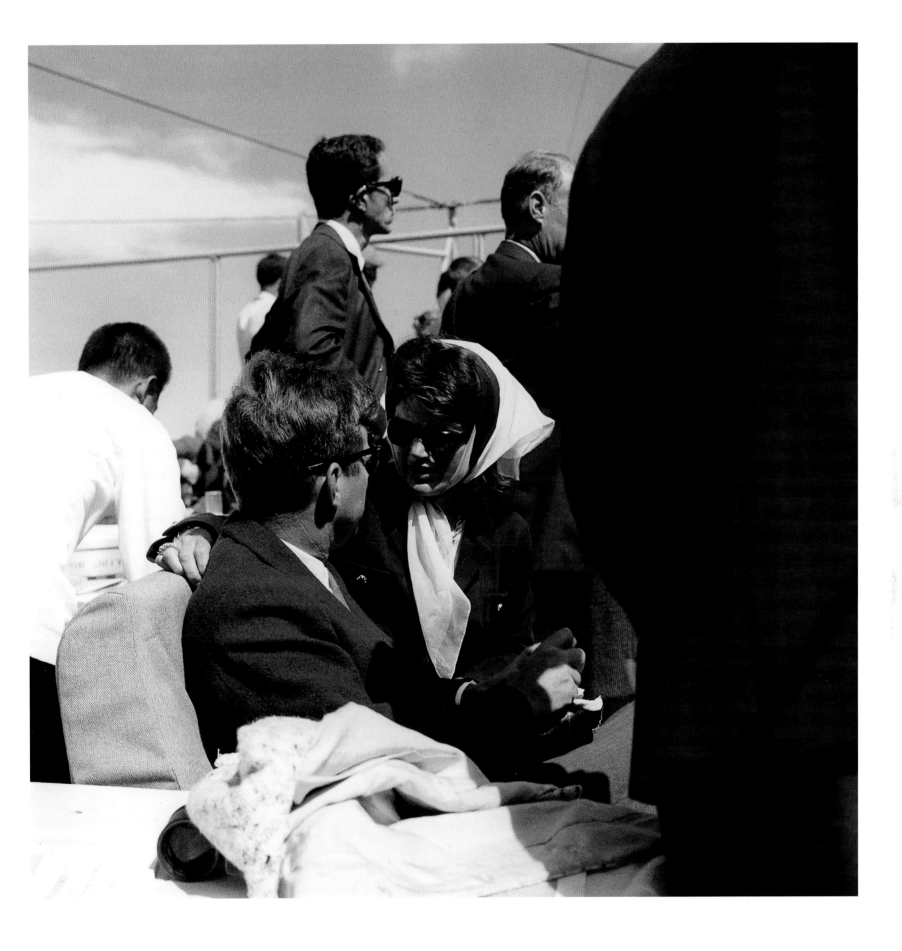

August 26, 1962 / Newport, RI / President Kennedy sails in Narragansett Bay on board the United States Coast Guard yacht *Manitou*

1962 / Hyannis Port, MA / President Kennedy with family on board the *Manitou*

August 11, 1962 / Newport, RI / President Kennedy with brother-in-law Peter Lawford aboard the United States Coast Guard yacht *Manitou*

September 22, 1962 / Newport, RI / President Kennedy with White House Press Secretary Pierre Salinger during the 21st America's Cup Race

August 1962 / Hyannis Port, MA / President Kennedy on his sailboat

August 1959 / Hyannis Port, MA / Senator Kennedy with family, sailing

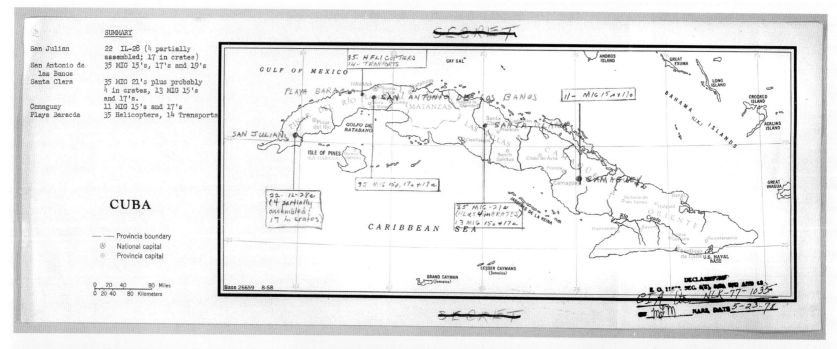

SUMMARY

San Julian	22 IL-28 (4 partially assembled; 17 in crates)
San Antonio de las Banos	35 MIG 15's, 17's and 19's
Santa Clara	35 MIG 21's plus probably 4 in crates, 13 MIG 15's and 17's.
Camaguey	11 MIG 15's and 17's
Playa Baracda	35 Helicopters, 14 Transports

CUBA

— — — Provincia boundary
⊛ National capital
⊙ Provincia capital

0 20 40   80 Miles
0 20 40   80 Kilometers

Base 26659 8-58

John F. Kennedy

Report to the American people, October 22, 1962

It shall be the policy of this nation to regard any nuclear missile launched from Cuba against any nation in the western hemisphere as an attack by the Soviet Union on the United States, requiring a full retaliatory response upon the Soviet Union...

My fellow citizens: let no one doubt that this is a difficult and dangerous effort ... No one can foresee precisely what course it will take or what costs or casualties will be incurred... But the greatest danger of all would be to do nothing... Our goal is not the victory of might, but the vindication of right – not peace at the expense of freedom, but both peace and freedom, here in this hemisphere, and, we hope around the world. God willing, that goal will be achieved.

Fidel Castro

to Nikita S. Khrushchev, October 26, 1962

From an analysis of the situation and reports in our possession, I consider that the aggression is almost imminent within the next twenty-four or seventy-two hours.

If ... the imperialists invade Cuba with the goal of occupying it, the danger that that aggressive policy possesses for humanity is so great that following that event the Soviet Union must never allow the circumstances in which the imperialists could launch the first nuclear strike against it...

That would be the moment [for the Soviet Union] to eliminate such danger forever through an act of clear legitimate defense, however harsh and terrible the solution would be, for there is no other.

Nikita S. Khrushchev

to John F. Kennedy, October 26, 1962

Mr. President, I appeal to you to weigh carefully what the aggressive, piratical actions which you have announced the United States intends to carry out in international waters would lead to...

If you have not lost command of yourself and realize clearly what this could lead to, then, Mr. President, you and I should not now pull on the ends of the rope in which you have tied a knot of war, because the harder you and I pull, the tighter this knot will become. And a time may come when this knot is tied so tight that the person who tied it is no longer capable of untying it, and then the knot will have to be cut. What that would mean I need not explain to you, because you yourself understand perfectly what dread forces our two countries possess.

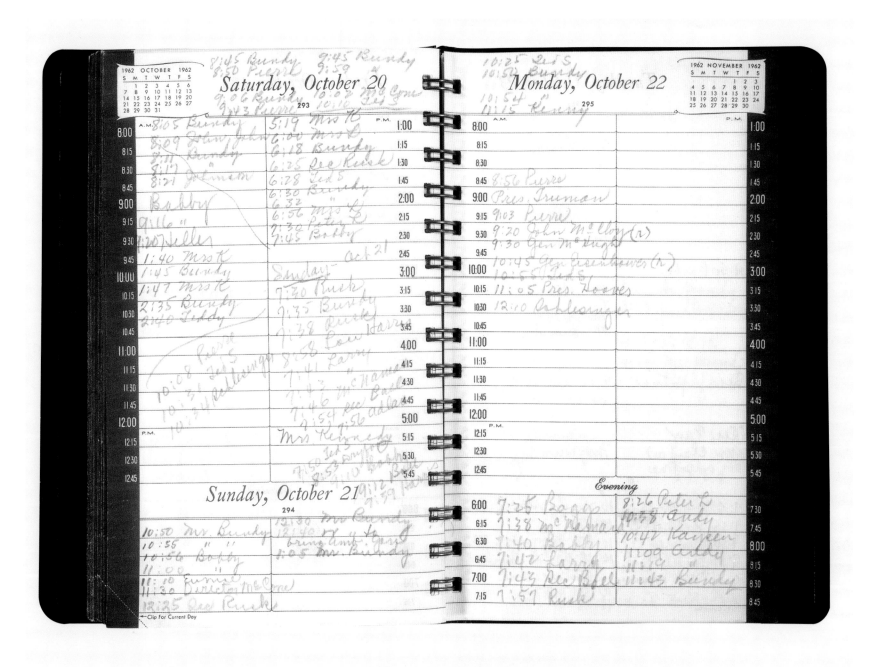

October 22, 1962 / Cuba airfield map at the time of the Cuban Missile Crisis
October 22, 1962 / President Kennedy's diary held by his secretary, Evelyn Lincoln

209

October 29, 1962 / Washington, DC / Executive Committee meeting at the White House during the Cuban Missile Crisis

October 29, 1962 / Washington, DC / President Kennedy confers with Secretary of Defense Robert McNamara in the West Wing colonnade at the White House during the Cuban Missile Crisis

October 3, 1962 / Washington, DC / President Kennedy confers with Attorney General Robert Kennedy in the West Wing colonnade at the White House

October 29, 1962 / Washington, DC / President Kennedy confers with Secretary of Defense Robert McNamara and General Maxwell Taylor (Chairman of the Joint Chiefs of Staff) in the West Wing colonnade at the White House during the Cuban Missile Crisis

January 25, 1963 / Washington, DC / Gathering of the Executive Committee at the White House: President Kennedy, General Maxwell Taylor, Chairman of the Joint Chiefs of Staff, and Robert McNamara, Secretary of Defense

513 State Street
Mishawaka Indiana
October 27, 1962

Dear President Kennedy,

Of course you are a busy man, but I just wanted to send you this letter to cheer you up a little. We are praying that all your decisions will be right. Everybody is hoping that we will have peace. We know that the situation is critical, however, we have confidence in you. God bless you daily.

A young citizen,
Betsy Pieters
St. Joseph School
10 years old

October 27, 1962 / Letter sent to the President by a ten-year-old pupil during the Cuban Missile Crisis

December 29, 1962 / Miami, FL / President Kennedy and Jacqueline talking to returning members of the 2506 Brigade at the Orange Bowl Stadium. Twenty months after the American-trained Cuban fighters were captured at the Bay of Pigs, Fidel Castro released them in return for $53 million in pharmaceuticals, baby food, farm equipment, and other goods prohibited by the US trade boycott of Cuba

December 2, 1961 / Philadelphia, PA / President Kennedy at the Army vs. Navy football game accompanied by Captain Tazewell Shepard and others. The first such match was held in Philadelphia's Franklin Field in 1899

October 10, 1962 / Washington, DC / President Kennedy claps his hands while daughter Caroline and son John, Jr., play in the Oval Office

November 27, 1962 / Washington, DC / John, Jr., and Caroline playing together during their birthday party at the White House. Their birthdays were celebrated together that year. They were born on November 25 and 27 respectively

October 31, 1963 / Washington, DC / A Halloween visit in the Oval Office from Caroline and John, Jr.

May 30, 1963 / Washington, DC / President Kennedy and John, Jr., in the President's secretary's office just prior to leaving for Memorial Day ceremonies at Arlington National Cemetery. Others in the room include the President's secretary, Evelyn Lincoln, and the President's Naval Aide, Captain Tazewell Shepard

"CHILDREN ARE THE WORLD'S MOST VALUABLE RESOURCE AND ITS BEST HOPE FOR THE FUTURE."

President Kennedy / July 25, 1963 / New York, NY / Address at UNICEF

November 27, 1962 / Washington, DC / John, Jr., and Caroline during their birthday party at the White House

1962 / Washington, DC / President Kennedy, Jacqueline Kennedy, Prince and Princess Radziwill celebrate Christmas with their children

January 6, 1963 / Hyannis Port, MA / President Kennedy and his wife during a weekend at Hyannis Port. Jackie's sister Princess Radziwill with her husband sit in the back

January 17, 1963 / Washington, DC / President Kennedy, the First Lady and the Prime Minister of Italy at the White House

December 29, 1962 / Miami, FL / President Kennedy and Mrs. Kennedy board a helicopter to travel from Miami, where they addressed Brigade 2506, to a press conference in Palm Beach, Florida

December 22, 1961 / Kindley, Bermuda / President Kennedy departs Kindley Air Force Base for Palm Beach, Florida, to meet his Argentinian counterpart

"IN THE LONG HISTORY OF THE WORLD, ONLY A FEW GENERATIONS HAVE BEEN GRANTED THE ROLE OF DEFENDING FREEDOM IN ITS HOUR OF MAXIMUM DANGER. I DO NOT SHRINK FROM THIS RESPONSIBILITY – I WELCOME IT."

President Kennedy / January 20, 1961 / Washington, DC / Inaugural address

January 14, 1963 / Washington, DC / President Kennedy delivers his State of the Union Address before Congress

March 28, 1963 / Washington, DC /
President Kennedy with Attorney
General Robert Kennedy at the
White House

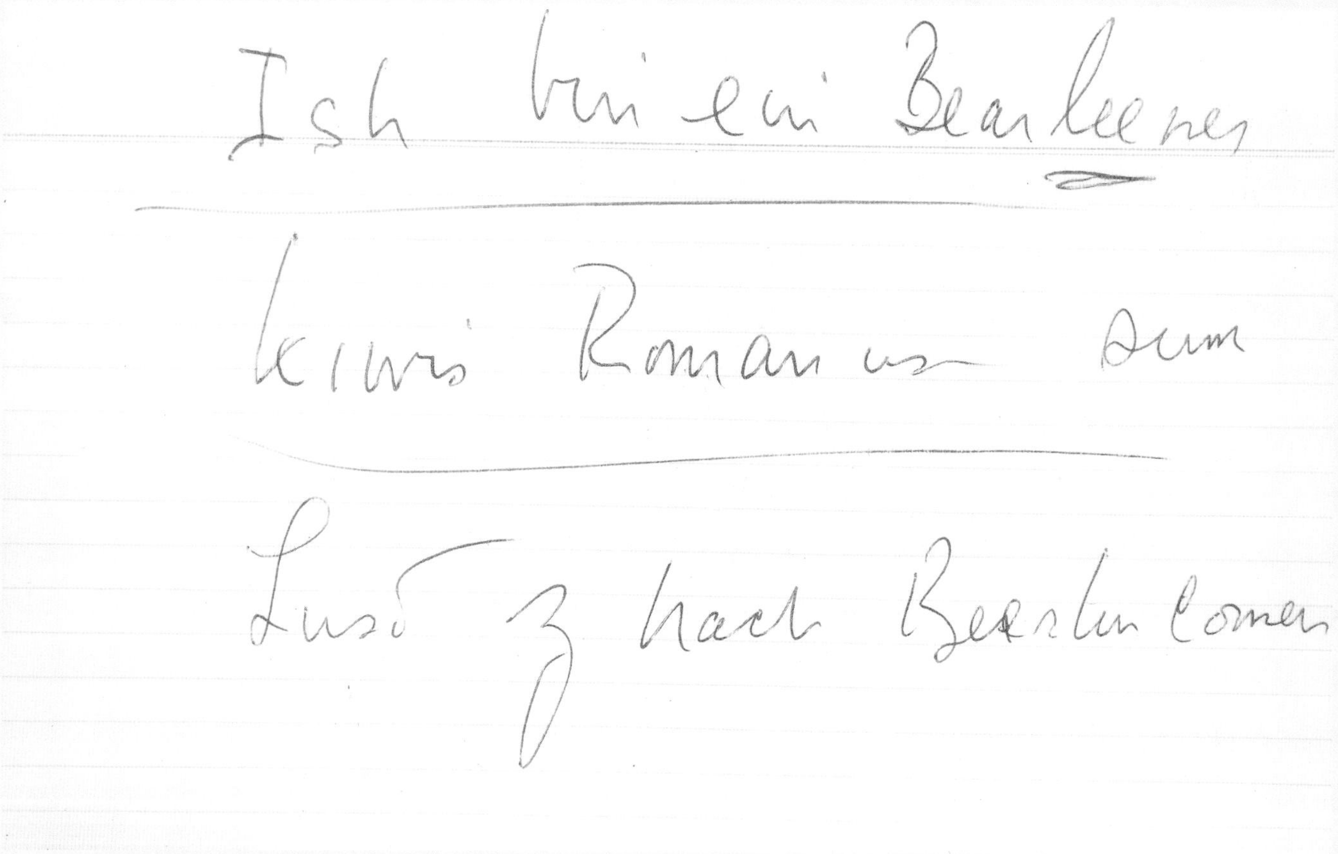

Ish bin ein Bearleener

kiwis Romanus um

Lust z nach Beerlin comen

June 26, 1963 / Pronunciation card for the Berlin Wall speech written by President Kennedy ("Ich bin ein Berliner")

July 2, 1963 / Naples, Italy / President Kennedy drives to the airport after visiting Italian President Segni and NATO officials

PAGES 232, 233:
August 23, 1963 / Otis Air Force Base, MA / John, Jr., running to greet his father, as the President arrives to join his family at Cape Cod
June 6, 1961 / Andrews Air Force Base, DC / Arrival of President Kennedy at Andrews upon his return from Europe

"WHAT REALLY COUNTS IS NOT THE IMMEDIATE ACT OF COURAGE OR OF VALOR, BUT THOSE WHO BEAR THE STRUGGLE DAY IN AND DAY OUT – NOT THE SUNSHINE PATRIOTS BUT THOSE WHO ARE WILLING TO STAND FOR A LONG PERIOD OF TIME."

President Kennedy / March 1, 1962 / White House / Address to members of the American Legion

June 6, 1963 / San Diego, CA / President Kennedy inspects the US Marine Guard on board the USS *Oriskany* off the coast of San Diego

June 11, 1963 / Washington, DC/ President Kennedy delivers his address on civil rights during the desegregation of the University of Alabama. "It ought to be possible ... for every American to enjoy the privileges of being American without regard to his race or color."

June 10, 1963 / Washington, DC / President Kennedy signing the Equal Pay Act, surrounded by representatives from women's rights associations. At the White House he said that the Equal Pay Act was basic to democracy, giving women the same rights in the workplace that they had enjoyed at the polling station since 1919

March 18, 1963 / Palm Beach, FL / President Kennedy departs West Palm Beach, Florida, for San Jose, Costa Rica

May 11, 1963 / Hyannis Port, MA / President Kennedy during a series of meetings with the Prime Minister of Canada Lester B. Pearson

July 24, 1963 / Washington, DC / Bill Clinton meets President Kennedy at Boys Nation in the Rose Garden of the White House. Boys Nation is a week-long program that teaches federal government practices to high school juniors

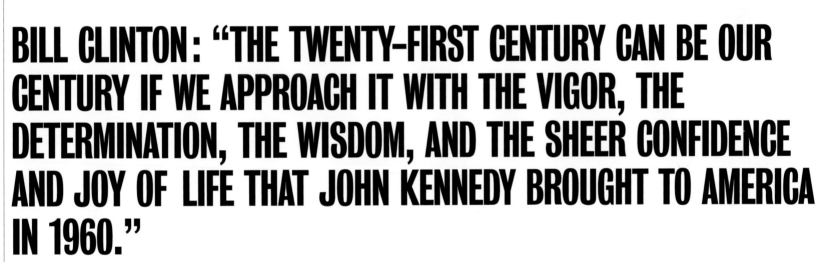

BILL CLINTON: "THE TWENTY-FIRST CENTURY CAN BE OUR CENTURY IF WE APPROACH IT WITH THE VIGOR, THE DETERMINATION, THE WISDOM, AND THE SHEER CONFIDENCE AND JOY OF LIFE THAT JOHN KENNEDY BROUGHT TO AMERICA IN 1960."

President Clinton / October 28, 1993 / Boston, MA / Address at the JFK Library

August 4, 1963 / Hyannis Port, MA / President Kennedy kisses his father Joseph on the porch

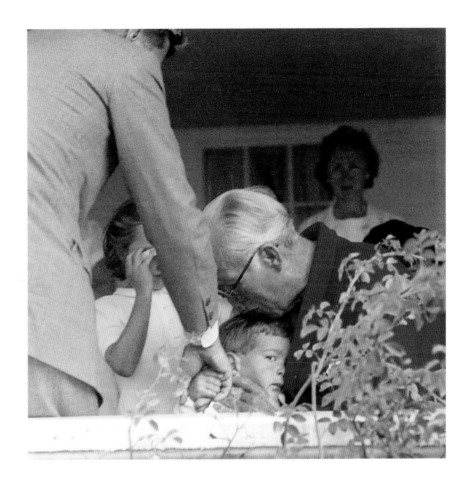

August 4, 1963 / Hyannis Port, MA / Joseph Kennedy kisses his grandson John, Jr., on the porch

August 26, 1963 / Cape Cod, MA / President Kennedy prepares to leave Cape Cod for Washington, via Otis Air Force Base

August 3, 1963 / Hyannis Port, MA / From left to right, are Kathleen Kennedy who is holding Christopher Kennedy, and Joseph P. Kennedy II. In front of Kathleen and Joseph are Ted Kennedy, Jr., and Kara Kennedy (partially hidden). In foreground, in front of Ted and Kara, walking away, is John F. Kennedy, Jr., Robert F. Kennedy, Jr., David Kennedy, Caroline B. Kennedy, President Kennedy, Michael Kennedy, Courtney Kennedy, Kerry Kennedy, Bobby Shriver, who is holding Tim Shriver (in a sailor suit), Maria Shriver (partially hidden) and Steve Smith, Jr. In front of Steve Smith, Jr., is Willam Smith (crying), Chris Lawford, Victoria Lawford, and Sydney Lawford

August 14, 1963 / Squaw Island off Hyannis Port, MA / President Kennedy and Jacqueline with their children, John, Jr., and Caroline. The dogs are: Clipper (standing), Charlie (with Caroline), Wolf (reclining), Shannon (with John, Jr.), and two of Pushinka's puppies (with Mrs. Kennedy)

August 31, 1963 / Hyannis Port, MA / President Kennedy and John, Jr., in town during the Labor Day weekend

August 31, 1963 / Hyannis Port, MA / President Kennedy relaxes on a boat off Hyannis Port during Labor Day weekend

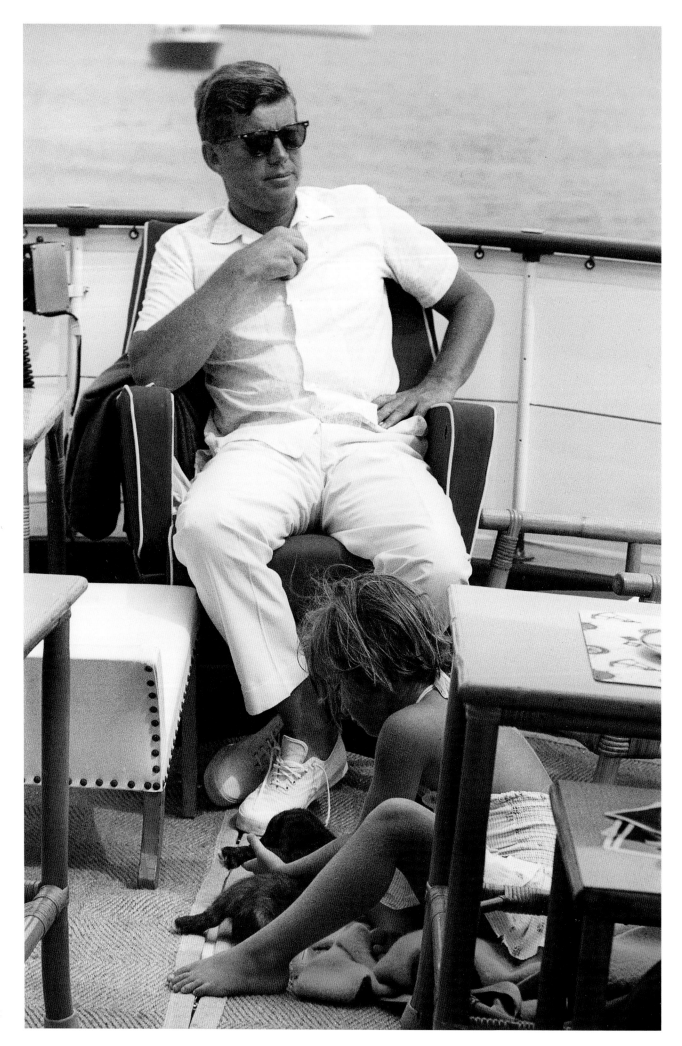

August 4, 1963 / Hyannis Port, MA / President
Kennedy with Caroline on *Honey Fitz*

August 4, 1963 / Hyannis Port, MA / Jackie
Kennedy during a weekend on board *Honey Fitz*

August 31, 1963 / Hyannis Port, MA / President Kennedy relaxes on board *Honey Fitz* off Hyannis Port during Labor Day weekend
August 31, 1963 / Hyannis Port, MA / John, Jr., plays with Sport Counselor Sandy Eiler

August 25, 1963 / Hyannis Port, MA / Caroline Kennedy sunbathing on the deck of *Honey Fitz*
July 28, 1963 / Hyannis Port, MA / Caroline Kennedy with her cousin, Maria Shriver, during a weekend

August 31, 1963 / Hyannis Port, MA / President Kennedy with daughter Caroline on board *Honey Fitz* during Labor Day weekend

August 4, 1963 / Hyannis Port, MA / A pregnant Jackie Kennedy during a weekend on board *Honey Fitz*

August 25, 1963 / Hyannis Port, MA /
President Kennedy relaxes on board
Honey Fitz

August 31, 1963 / Hyannis Port, MA /
A pregnant Jackie Kennedy during
Labor Day weekend on board *Honey Fitz*

August 25, 1963 / Hyannis Port, MA / President Kennedy sailing with Caroline Kennedy
July 28, 1963 / Hyannis Port, MA / President Kennedy with Caroline on board *Honey Fitz* with Maria Shriver (left)

DANGER
KEEP AWAY

May 10, 1963 / Hyannis Port, MA / View of the Kennedy estate on the day that the President receives the Prime Minister of Canada Lester B. Pearson

September 2, 1963 / Hyannis Port, MA / CBS News anchor Walter Cronkite interviews President Kennedy over Labor Day weekend to inaugurate the first half-hour network national nightly news broadcast

September 24, 1963 / Ashland, WI / President Kennedy on his Conservation Tour at the Ashland-Bayfield County Airport before heading on to Duluth, Minnesota. Throwing his head back in laughter is Secretary of the Interior Stewart Udall

September 24, 1963 / Duluth, MN / President Kennedy delivering a speech at the Land and People's Conference, during his Conservation Tour

PEOPLE CONFE
GRE
S RE
SEAL OF THE PRESIDENT OF THE UNITED STATES

"ALL OF US DO NOT HAVE EQUAL TALENT, BUT ALL OF US SHOULD HAVE AN EQUAL OPPORTUNITY TO DEVELOP OUR TALENTS."

President Kennedy / June 6, 1963 / Address at San Diego University

September 25, 1963 / Billings, MT / A girl is lifted above a fence to be kissed by President Kennedy during the Conservation Tour in the West

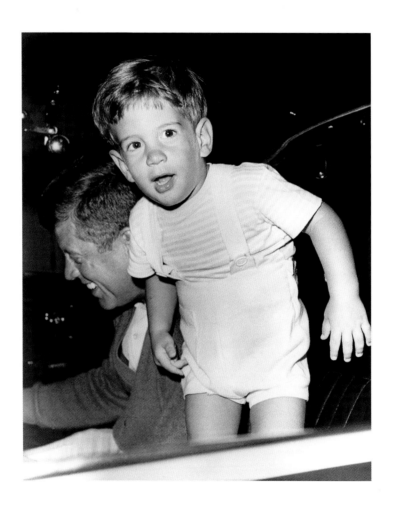

August 12, 1963 / Hyannis Port, MA / President Kennedy with John, Jr.
October 10, 1963 / Washington, DC / President Kennedy with John, Jr., in the West Wing colonnade at the White House

October 10, 1963 / Washington, DC /
President Kennedy with John, Jr.,
in the West Wing colonnade at the White
House

October 17, 1963 / Washington, DC / President Kennedy with John, Jr., in the Oval Office

May 21, 1963 / Washington, DC / Jackie Kennedy with John, Jr., at the ceremony honoring astronaut Gordon Cooper at the White House

October 17, 1963 / Hyannis Port, MA / Jacqueline Kennedy and her children return from their European vacation

November 21, 1963 / San Antonio, TX / President Kennedy during his last trip to Texas

November 22, 1963 / Fort Worth, TX / Crowd cheers President Kennedy during his last Conservation Tour in Texas

1963 / Washington, DC / President
Kennedy with aides at the White House
1969 / Official (posthumous) portrait of
President John F. Kennedy by Aaron Shikler

1961 / Washington, DC / President Kennedy
at a Cabinet meeting

1961 / Washington, DC / President Kennedy at a Cabinet meeting
1961 / Washington, DC / President Kennedy during a Cabinet meeting with Secretary of the Interior Stewart Udall, speechwriter and presidential advisor Ted Sorensen, and other members of the Cabinet

I HAVE A RENDEZVOUS WITH DEATH

By Alan Seeger (1888–1916)

I have a rendezvous with Death
At some disputed barricade,
When Spring comes back with rustling shade
And apple-blossoms fill the air —
I have a rendezvous with Death
When Spring brings back blue days and fair.

It may be he shall take my hand
And lead me into his dark land
And close my eyes and quench my breath —
It may be I shall pass him still.
I have a rendezvous with Death
On some scarred slope of battered hill,
When Spring comes round again this year
And the first meadow-flowers appear.

God knows 'twere better to be deep
Pillowed in silk and scented down,
Where Love throbs out in blissful sleep,
Pulse nigh to pulse, and breath to breath,
Where hushed awakenings are dear...
But I've a rendezvous with Death
At midnight in some flaming town,
When Spring trips north again this year,
And I to my pledged word am true,
I shall not fail that rendezvous.

November 22, 1963

November 22, 1963 / Dallas, TX / Jacqueline Kennedy at Love Field airport, a few hours after the assassination, getting in the plane taking her back to Washington

November 22, 1963 / On board Air Force One between Dallas and Washington / Swearing-in ceremony, Lyndon B. Johnson becomes the thirty-sixth president of the United States

November 24, 1963 / Washington, DC / Sunlight streams through the columns of the Rotunda of the US Capitol, onto the coffin of the late President Kennedy. The body of the President would lie in state in the Rotunda until funeral services the next day

November 25, 1963 / Washington, DC / Jacqueline Kennedy, John, Jr., and Caroline leave the White House for a service at the Capitol, honoring President Kennedy. Behind Jacqueline Kennedy is Attorney General Robert Kennedy. Peter Lawford, John F. Kennedy's brother-in-law, is at the far left

November 25, 1963 / Washington, DC / President Kennedy's funeral. The flag that covered the coffin has been ceremoniously removed and presented to Jacqueline Kennedy

THE UNDELIVERED SPEECH

(...) America today is stronger than ever before.
Our adversaries have not abandoned their ambitions —
our dangers have not diminished — our vigilance
cannot be relaxed. But now we have the military,
the scientific and the economic strength to do whatever
must be done for the preservation and promotion of freedom.

That strength will never be used in pursuit of aggressive
ambitions — it will always be used in pursuit of peace.
It will never be used to promote provocations — it will always
be used to promote the peaceful settlement of disputes.

We in this country, in this generation, are — by destiny rather
than choice — the watchmen on the walls of world freedom.
We ask, therefore, that we may be worthy of our power
and responsibility — that we may exercise our strength
with wisdom and restraint — and that we may achieve
in our time and for all time the ancient vision of "peace
on earth, good will toward men." That must always be
our goal — and the righteousness of our cause must
always underlie our strength. For as was written long ago :
"Except the Lord keep the city, the watchman waketh but in vain."

President John F. Kennedy / November 22, 1963 / Dallas, TX / Speech prepared for delivery at the Trade Mart

1987 / Arlington, VA / President Kennedy's tomb in Arlington Cemetery with its eternal flame

1960 / Caroline Kennedy proudly displays her father's portrait

Joseph Patrick Kennedy (1888–1969) — married 1914 — **Rose Elizabeth Fitzgerald (1890–1995)**

Joseph Patrick Kennedy Jr. (1915–1944)	John Fitzgerald Kennedy (1917–1963)	Rosemary Kennedy (1918–)	Kathleen "Kick" Kennedy (1920–1948)	Eunice Mary Kennedy (1921–)	Patricia Kennedy (1924–)	Robert Francis "Bob" Kennedy (1925–1968)	Jean Ann Kennedy (1928–)	Edward Moore Kennedy (1932–)
	married 1953		married 1944	married 1953	married 1954	married 1950	married 1956	married 1958
	Jacqueline Lee Bouvier (1929–1994)		William John R. Cavendish (1917–1944)	Robert Sargent Shriver Jr. (1915–)	Peter Lawford (1923–1984)	Ethel Skakel (1928–)	Stephen Edward Smith (1927–1990)	Virginia Joan Bennett (1936–)
	Caroline Bouvier Kennedy (1957–)			Robert Sargent Shriver III (1954–)	Christopher Lawford (1955–)	Kathleen Harlington Kennedy (1951–)	Stephen E. Smith Jr. (1957–)	Kara A. Kennedy (1960–)
	John Fitzgerald Kennedy J.-R. (1960-1999)			Maria Owings Shriver (1955–)	Sydney M. Lawford (1956–)	Joseph P. Kennedy II (1952–)	William Kennedy Smith (1960–)	Edward M. Kennedy Jr. (1961–)
	Patrick Bouvier Kennedy (August 5–7, 1963)			Timothy Perry Shriver (1959–)	Victoria Lawford (1958–)	Robert F. Kennedy Jr. (1954–)	Amanda Mary Smith (1967–)	Patrick J. Kennedy (1967–)
				Mark Kennedy Shriver (1964–)	Robin Lawford (1961–)	David A. Kennedy (1955–1984)	Kym Maria Smith (1972–)	
				Anthony Paul Shriver (1965–)		Mary C. Kennedy (1956–)		
						Michael Lemoyne Kennedy (1958–1997)		
						Mary K. Kennedy (1959–)		
						Christopher G. Kennedy (1963–)		
						Matthew M. Taylor Kennedy (1965–)		
						Douglas Harriman Kennedy (1967–)		
						Rory E. Kennedy (1968–)		

Index

Page numbers refer to introductory text and picture captions.

2506 Brigade 216

Acapulco 9
Air Force One 13, 124, 289
Alliance for Progress 178
American Legion 234
American University, The, Washington DC 52
America's Cup Race 171, 200, 205
Amherst College, Amherst, MA 168
Anacostia, DC: Naval Air Station 48
Andrews Air Force Base, DC 231
Apollo project 11
Arlington National Cemetery 13, 218, 297
arms race 10
Armstrong, Neil 11
Army vs. Navy football games 217
Ashland-Bayfield County Airport, WI 264
Austin, TX 13
Ayub Khan, President Mohammad 185

Bailey's Beach, Newport 150
Bartlett, Charles 9
Bay of Pigs, Cuba 11, 216
Beale, Sir Howard 171
Berlin 11-12
Berlin Wall 11, 230
Billings, Lemoyne 7, 8, 16
Billings, MT 267
Boston, MA 7, 9, 15, 16, 28, 29, 36, 39, 42, 45, 49, 51, 57, 58, 65, 68, 72, 86
  Evacuation Day Parade 50
Bourguiba, President Habib 114
Boys Nation 240
Braun, Dr. Wernher von 149
Breakers, Newport, The 171
Brigade 2506 224
Brookline district, Boston 7
Buckingham Palace, London 27

Callas, Maria 172
Camp David, MD 198
Cape Canaveral, FL 13, 147, 149
Cape Cod, MA 231, 244
Capodochino airport, Italy 182
Carcassonne, France 24
Casals, Pablo 140
Castro, Fidel 11, 208, 216
CBS News 263
Charlie (dog) 246
Chaterji, Hon. D.N. 177
Chicago, IL 93
Chicago White Sox 116, 117
Choate College for boys, CT 7, 17
Churchill, Sir Winston 106
Clinton, President Bill 240, 241
Clipper (dog) 246
Cold War 10, 12
Columbia Trust 7
Conklin, Captain F.L. 39
Connally, Governor John 13
Connolly, Edward 50
Conservation Tour (1963) 264, 267, 277
Cooper, Gordon 274
Cronkite, Walter 263
Cuban Missile Crisis 11, 181, 208-11, 213, 215

Dallas, TX 13, 296
Democratic Party 10, 65, 88, 93, 106, 174
Dexter School, Boston, MA 18, 20
Dublin 12
Duluth, MN 264

Eiler, Sandy 252
Eisenhower, President Dwight 9

Elizabeth, Queen (later the Queen Mother) 27
Elizabeth II, Queen 9
Elysée Palace, France 123
Equal Pay Act 237

Figaro, Le 119
Ford Motor Company: presidential limousine 184
Fort Worth, TX 13, 277
Foster, Secret Service agent 198
Frost, Robert 168
Funke, Captain 48

Gaulle, President Charles de 123
George VI, King 27
George Washington University 9
Georgetown, Washington, DC 83
Giscard d'Estaing, Valéry 176
Glen Ora, Middleburg, VA 107
Glenn, Colonel John 147
Grace, Princess, of Monaco 173
Griffiths Stadium, DC 116, 117

Hague, Netherlands, The 27
Hammersmith Farms, RI 54
Harvard University 8, 19, 32, 72
Henry Ford Museum, Dearborn, MI 184
Hitler, Adolf 8
Honey Fitz 150, 251, 257-60
Hoover, Herbert 60
House of Representatives 9
Hyannis Port, Cape Cod 7, 16, 40-42, 44, 57, 128-30, 174, 195, 197, 198, 203, 206, 207, 222, 239, 242, 243, 248-52, 255-60, 262, 263, 268, 275

Instituto Nacional de Protección a la Infancia, Mexico City 189
Ireland, visit to (1963) 12
Italy, Prime Minister of 223

J Six ranch, Arizona 7
Jackson, Senator 58
Japan, Prime Minister of 123
JFK Library, Boston 241
Johnson, President Lyndon B. 13, 109, 184, 190, 289

Kennedy, Caroline (daughter) 9, 107, 150, 193, 195, 197, 198, 218, 220, 245, 246, 250, 255, 256, 260, 294, 299
Kennedy, Christopher 245
Kennedy, Courtney 245
Kennedy, David 245
Kennedy, Edward Moore (brother) 7, 44-6, 53, 77, 110, 129, 174
Kennedy, Eunice Mary (sister) 7, 16, 27, 35, 44, 45, 53
Kennedy, Jacqueline Bouvier (Jackie; later Onassis; wife) 107, 114, 128, 133, 150, 185, 190, 193, 195, 197, 200, 221-4, 246, 251, 257, 274, 275
  meets JFK 9
  journalism career 9
  marries JFK 9, 53, 54
  children 9, 10, 12
  Presidential campaign 102
  European tour (1961) 119, 120, 123, 124
  in Venezuela 144, 145
  visits India 152-4, 156, 157
  Mona Lisa exhibition 165, 166, 169
  sees Mr. President 188
  in Mexico City 189
  JFK's assassination 13, 288
  JFK's funeral 13, 294, 295
Kennedy, Jean Ann (sister) 7, 44, 45, 53
Kennedy, John Fitzgerald
  family tree 301
  birth (May 29 1917) 7
  health 7
  childhood 7, 16

education 7, 8, 17-21, 32
  back condition 8, 9
  travels abroad 8, 22-7
  war service 8, 36, 39, 84
  election as a congressman 9, 42, 49
  successful Senate campaign 9, 51
  meets Jackie 9, 53
  marries Jackie 9, 53, 54
  Pulitzer Prize 9, 62, 63
  campaigns for nomination as vice president 65
  re-election as Senator 67
  fights against racial segregation 9, 11, 236
  "Rackets Committee" 9, 69
  Presidential election 10, 64, 84-7, 90, 93, 94, 97, 98, 100, 102-5
  takes oath of office (1961) 109
  inaugural speech 109
  European tour (1961) 119-21, 123, 124, 126
  in Venezuela 145
  Alliance for Progress plan 178
  in Mexico City 178, 189
  creation of Peace Corps (1961) 11, 186
  Bay of Pigs fiasco (1961) 11, 216
  meeting with Khrushchev (1961) 11
  Cuban Missile Crisis 11, 181, 208, 209, 211, 215
  Berlin visit (1963) 11-12
  visits Ireland (1963) 12
  signs Nuclear Test Ban Treaty (1963) 12
  assassinated (November 22, 1963) 13, 288
  lies in state 290, 293
  funeral 13, 290, 293
  his tomb in Arlington Cemetery 297
  Warren Commission investigations 13
  Profiles in Courage 9, 62, 63
  Why England Slept 8
Kennedy, John Fitzgerald, Jr. (son) 10, 132, 150, 195-8, 218, 220, 231, 243, 245, 246, 248, 252, 268, 270, 273, 294
Kennedy, Joseph Patrick (father) 7, 8, 29, 31, 44, 45, 242, 243
Kennedy, Joseph Patrick, II 245
Kennedy, Joseph Patrick, Jr. (brother) 7, 8, 9, 16, 29, 31, 35, 36
Kennedy, Kara 245
Kennedy, Kathleen ("Kick"; sister) 7, 16, 35, 40, 41, 44, 245
Kennedy, Kerry 245
Kennedy, Michael 245
Kennedy, Patricia (sister) 7, 45, 53
Kennedy, Patrick Bouvier (son) 12
Kennedy, Robert Francis ("Bob"; brother) 7, 9-11, 16, 27, 31, 44-6, 53, 54, 69, 74, 77, 80, 110, 111, 174, 212, 228, 294
Kennedy, Robert Francis, Jr. 245
Kennedy, Rose Elizabeth (née Fitzgerald; mother) 7, 35, 44, 45
Kennedy, Rosemary (sister) 7, 16
Kennedy, Ted, Jr. 245
Kennedy, Virginia (sister-in-law) 129
Kennedy Space Center, Cape Canaveral 13, 147
Khrushchev, Nikita 11, 126, 208
Kindley Air Force Base, Bermuda 225
King, Reverend Martin Luther, Jr. 10
Krim, Arthur 172

La Morita, Venezuela 144, 145
Lake Pichola, Udaipur, India 153, 157
Land and People's Conference (1963) 264
Laos 11
Lawford, Chris 245
Lawford, Peter (brother-in-law) 76, 204, 294
Lawford, Sydney 245
Lawford, Victoria 245
Leonardo da Vinci: Mona Lisa 165, 166
Lincoln, President Abraham 11
Lincoln, Evelyn 90, 209, 218
Lodge, Henry Cabot, Jr. 9
London 8, 22, 27, 31, 35, 36
London School of Economics 7
López Mateos, Adolfo 178

Los Angeles, CA 88, 106
Louvre, Paris 165, 166
Love Field airport, Dallas 288
Lyautey, Marshal 14

McClellan Committee 69
McMahon, Patrick 8
McNamara, Robert 211, 214
Madison Square Garden, New York 174
Malraux, André 165, 166, 169
Manhattan, New York 102
Manitou (US Coast Guard yacht) 202, 203, 204
Marciano, Rocky 60
Memorial Coliseum, Los Angeles 106
Mexico City 178, 189
Miami, FL 216, 224
Mona Lisa exhibition, National Gallery of Art, New York 165, 166, 169
Monroe, Marilyn 172, 174
Mr. President (film) 188
Mt Vesuvius, Italy 23
Munich treaty (1938) 8
Muñoz Marin, Luis 140
Mussolini, Benito 8

Naples, Italy 182, 231
Narragansett Bay, Newport, RI 150, 202
NASA 147
National Guard 11
National Guard Armory, Washington, DC 170
NATO 231
Nehru, Prime Minister Jawaharlal 154, 156, 177
New Delhi, India 154, 156
New York, NY 67, 73, 98, 102, 143, 165, 172, 174, 219
Newport, RI 9, 53, 54, 150, 171, 196, 200, 202, 204, 205
Nixon, Richard 10, 60, 93
Nuclear Test Ban Treaty (1963) 12
Nuremberg, Germany 23

Orange Bowl Stadium, Miami, FL 216
Oriskany, USS 235
Oswald, Lee Harvey 13
Otis Air Force Base, MA 151, 231, 244

Palais de Chaillot, Paris 120
Palm Beach, FL 13, 16, 46, 74, 77, 224, 225, 238
Paris, France 119, 165
Parkland Memorial Hospital, Dallas 13
Patiala, Maharaja of 154
Peace Corps 11, 186
Pearson, Lester B. 239, 262
Peter Brent Brigham hospital, Boston 7
Philadelphia, PA 217
PT-109 (torpedo boat) 8, 39
Pushinka (dog) 246

Quonset Point Naval Air Station, RI 193

"Rackets Committee" 9, 69
Radziwill, Prince 221, 222
Radziwill, Princess Lee (sister-in-law) 151, 153, 157, 221, 222
Raherty, Hector 50
Republican Party 93
Rice University, TX 146
Rio de Janeiro, Brazil 35, 181

St Marys Church, Newport 54
St Matthews Cathedral, Washington 13
Salinger, Pierre 205
San Antonio, TX 13, 276
San Diego, CA 235
San Diego University 266
San Jose, Costa Rica 238

Santa Monica, CA 76
Saturn Launch System 149
Schärf, Adolph 126
Seamans, Robert 149
Second World War 8, 35, 84
Secret Service 198
Security & Exchange Commission (SEC) 8
Seeger, Alan: 'I have a rendezvous with death' 384
Segni, President Antonio 182, 231
Sékou Touré, President Ahmed 182
Shannon (dog) 246
Shepard, Alan 190
Shepard, Captain Tazewell 217, 218
Shikler, Aaron 279
Shriver, Bobby 245
Shriver, Maria 245, 255, 260
Shriver, Tim 245
Smith, Steve, Jr. 245
Smith, William 245
Sorensen, Ted 282
South Carolina 39
South Pacific 8, 39, 84
space travel 11, 146-9, 190
Springfield, OH 95
Squaw Island, off Hyannis Port 151, 246
Stanford Graduate School of Business 8
Stevenson, Adlai 65
Strategic Air Command, Offutt AFB, NE 58
Sukarno, President 115

Taj Mahal, Agra, India 152
Taylor, General Maxwell 213, 214
Tower, General 58
Trade Mart, Dallas 296
Truman, President Harry 58, 141

Udaipur, India 153, 154, 157
Udall, Stewart L. 264, 282
UNICEF 219
United Nations General Assembly, New York 143
University of Alabama 11, 236
University of Princeton 7
US Air Force 8
US Marine Corps 8
US Marine Guard 235
US Navy 8, 36, 39, 48
US State Department auditorium 158, 163

Vassar College, NY 9
Venezuela 144, 145
Venice, Italy 22, 23
Vienna, Austria 124, 126
Vietnam 112
Virginia 133

Warren Commission 13
Washington, DC 52, 60, 63, 67, 69, 79, 80, 82, 84, 90, 104, 105, 107, 109, 112-15, 123, 140-42, 163, 165, 166, 169, 170, 173, 176, 177, 182, 185, 186, 188, 190, 191, 195, 210-13, 218, 221, 227, 228, 240, 279, 294, 295
  Cabinet meetings 280, 282
  Capitol Building 13, 290, 293
  Congress 227
  Executive Committee meetings 210, 214
Washington Senators 116, 117
Washington Times Herald 9
White House, Washington 10, 11, 107, 110, 111, 115, 132, 134-42, 158, 165, 173, 177, 186, 190, 191, 214, 220, 223, 228, 234, 236, 237, 268, 270, 273, 274, 279
Wisconsin 103
Wittenberg College, Springfield, OH 95
Wolf (dog) 246

Authors' Acknowledgements

Pierre-Henri Verlhac dedicates this work to his wife Anne and his daughter to come.

Yann-Brice Dherbier dedicates this book to Axelle Emden and Chantal Dherbier. Thank you for your immense support.
You help me make my dreams come true every day.

The authors also would particularly like to thank
Corbis France photography agency for advice and assistance provided from the early stages of this project. Corbis carried out
detailed research among its Bettmann and Sygma collections and delivered archive images of the highest quality
and
The Atalante team, especially Xavier Barral and Stéphane Crémer, for their belief in this project from its inception,
their expert eye, and their continued involvement in this work
Diane Auberger, Marie-Christine Biebuyck, Elliott Erwitt, James B. Hill, Ron Sachs, Michael D. Shulman, Ann Vachon, and Antoine
Verdet for their invaluable help in locating and retrieving these images
Alice Marouani and Jacques Séguéla for their interest in our projects and their help in making them happen
Joe Consolazio, Thomas Couteau, Fabrice Fournier, and Edouard de Pouzilhac for their daily support and precious help
Gilles Amsallem, Christian Gambotti, Valérie de Laveaucoupet, and Pierre Vincent for their expert advice.

Picture Acknowledgements

Bettman/Corbis: 18, 20, 36, 76, 85, 93, 122, 150-151, 163, 173, 181, 192, 291; © Cornell Capa/Magnum Photos: 88, 90, 102-105, 280-283, 285; Geoffrey Clements/Corbis: 279; Corbis: 16 top right, 69, 121, 128-131, 195, 204; Corbis Sygma: 193, 203, 207; © Elliot Erwitt/Magnum Photos: 73, 89, 293, 295; Ford Motor Company/JFK Library, Boston: 184; © Arnold Frankel/JFK Library, Boston: 87; © Toni Frissell/Library of Congress/Magnum Photos: 55; Government of Udaipur: 157; © Erich Hartman/Magnum Photos: 297; JFK Library, Boston: 15, 16 top left, 16 bottom right, 17 top left, 17 right, 19, 21-30, 32-35, 39-51, 53-54, 57-58, 60-67, 79, 84, 86, 108, 125, 127, 145, 175, 208-209, 215, 230, 292; JFK Library/Courtesy of Princess Irena Galitzine: 133; Robert Knudsen, White House/JFK Library, Boston: 116-117, 134-139, 164-166, 182, 196, 200-202, 205-206, 218 bottom right, 225, 228-229, 231, 235, 269; Le Figaro: 118; Look Magazine/Douglas Jones: 56, 68, 70-71, 74-75, 77-78; Look Magazine/John Vachon: 80-83; NASA: 149; Genevieve Naylor/Corbis: 91; Abbie Rowe, National Park Service/JFK Library, Boston: 107, 112-115, 123, 142, 159-162, 167, 170, 176-177, 185, 188, 191, 217, 233, 236, 294; Ronald Sachs/Consolidated News: 240; Sargent Studios/JFK Library, Boston: 17 bottom left; Rowland Scherman, Peace Corps/JFK Library, Boston: 186-187; Sears/Pathe: 16 bottom left; Cecil Stoughton, White House/JFK Library, Boston: 110-111, 132, 140-141, 143, 147, 152-154, 169, 171-172, 174, 178-180, 183, 189-190, 197-199, 210-214, 216, 218 top left, 218 top right, 218 bottom left, 220, 222-224, 227, 232, 237-239, 242-265, 267-268, 270-271, 274-277, 288; Cecil W. Stoughton/Lyndon B. Johnson Library: 289; © Molley Thayer/Magnum Photos: 221; Stanley Tretick/Corbis Sygma: 92, 94, 96-99, 101, 194, 272-273, 278, 299; US Airforce: 59; US Army Signal Corps/JFK Library, Boston: 109; US Department of State: 119, 124, 126, 144; US Information Agency: 31; US Information Service: 155; US Information Service, India: 156; US Navy: 37.